God
Gave Me You

A True Story of Love, Loss, and a Heaven-Sent Miracle

Tricia Seaman

with Diane Nichols

HOWARD BOOKS
An Imprint of Simon & Schuster, Inc.
New York   Nashville   London   Toronto   Sydney   New Delhi

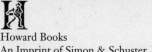

Howard Books
An Imprint of Simon & Schuster, Inc.
1230 Avenue of the Americas
New York, NY 10020

First Howard Books trade paperback edition April 2017

HOWARD and colophon are trademarks of Simon & Schuster, Inc.

For information about special discounts for bulk purchases, please contact Simon & Schuster Special Sales at 1-866-506-1949 or business@simonandschuster.com.

The Simon & Schuster Speakers Bureau can bring authors to your live event. For more information or to book an event, contact the Simon & Schuster Speakers Bureau at 1-866-248-3049 or visit our website at www.simonspeakers.com.

Interior design by Davina Mock-Maniscalco
Photos courtesy of the Seaman family

Manufactured in the United States of America

10   8   6   4   2   1   3   5   7   9

Library of Congress Cataloging-in-Publication Data

Names: Seaman, Tricia. Nichols, Diane, 1956–
Title: God gave me you : A true story of love, loss, and a heaven-sent miracle :
   a memoir / by Tricia Seaman ; with Diane Nichols.
Description: New York: Howard Books, 2016
Identifiers: LCCN 2015042617
Subjects: LCSH: Somers, Trish –2014. Cancer—Patients—Pennsylvania—Biography.
   Cancer—Patients—United States—Biography. Cancer—Patients—Family relation-
   ships.
Classification: LCC RC265.6.S67 S43 2016   DDC 362.19699/40092—dc23
LC record available at http://lccn.loc.gov/2015042617

ISBN 978-1-5011-3183-7
ISBN 978-1-5011-3195-0 (pbk)
ISBN 978-1-5011-3184-4 (ebook)

*This book is dedicated to and in loving memory
of my grandmother, Anna Dimm.*

*Thank you, Memaw, for teaching me kindness, gentleness,
and compassion. Your love influenced my life in ways that
will live on in my children and generations to come.*

*You were a truly beautiful person with a genuine spirit. I
will see you again one day. Until then . . . I love you more.*

Contents

Contents

Friday
October 18, 2013
2:02 a.m.

Wesley—

Here I am in the hospital thinking about you and missing you and wishing you were here to hug and hold. I hope that I will be around to see you grow up and become a wonderful man that I know you can and will be. I am proud of you and grateful that you have been a strong and big boy to have been able to accept the changes that you have been through over the last three years. Although I don't know what is to happen from here—at this point—I do know that I will try to do whatever I can to live as long as I can so that I can be with you. If I have to leave you, I will find someone for you to be with and be happy. Another big change in your life may be coming. But I know you will make it through!

I love you,
Mommy

Introduction

It was the Friday afternoon before Mother's Day when the school bus screeched to a halt in front of our house. I had just baked a fresh batch of chocolate chip cookies and was placing them on a plate to cool. The door slammed, and I heard the usual hustle and bustle of backpacks slung to the floor, but then little footsteps came up behind me.

"This is for you." Wesley held up a beautiful purple petunia planted in a clay pot, a rich shade of blue—my favorite color.

I paused, a bit stunned, then set down my spatula. "Is this a Mother's Day gift, for me?"

He nodded and grinned. "Yeah."

The combination of the purple flowers and blue pot was far from a coincidence.

"Thank you," I said, touched beyond measure. "It's perfect because blue is my favorite color and purple was your mommy's. Did you make this as a present for both of us?"

His grin broke into a full-blown smile. "Yep. That's why I picked those flowers out of all the kinds to choose from and the bright blue paint."

My heart pooled into a combination of love, surprise, and gratitude. So far, I had taken very cautious baby steps, helping him with his homework, tucking him into bed, packing his lunchbox, and seeing him blend in with my other children as they went off to school. I had read him stories, made sure he brushed his teeth—everything I did with my other kids. Yet I wondered if he would ever give me a sign that he felt safe enough to truly accept me, not as a caregiver or any kind of replacement, but as the second mother God chose for him after the only mother he had ever known had to leave him to go to heaven. Would he ever open his heart to me, as broken and shattered as it was? As I stood weak in the knees with this potted petunia cupped in my hands, I knew that was exactly what he just gifted me.

"I love it," I said, meaning it more than he knew. "And I'm sure that your mommy does, too." I swallowed back tears, gave him a huge hug, and kissed him on the top of his head. He smelled of shampoo and fresh country air.

"Where should we put it?" His gaze scanned the room.

"How about the windowsill above the sink?" I turned and placed it there in a golden patch of sunshine. "That way everyone can see it."

The other kids came barreling into the kitchen joining Wesley for some warm cookies and milk. As they laughed and talked, joked and giggled, I leaned against the counter and embraced every second to save as a beloved memory. This is one of the things this unexpected journey has taught me. Simple moments and family time are what the heart should hold on to. If you get too caught up in life's fast pace and trivial things, you could all too easily miss them. I took a moment to remember my promise to Wesley's mom, my beloved friend Trish—to tell her remarkable story. What were the chances I'd learn so many lessons from a brief encounter in a hospital room? Who would have guessed a stranger would enter my life and I would be forever changed as a mother, a nurse, a wife, and a person? What were the chances one "hello" could have led us all here and change my family forever? Then again, it wasn't chance at all and that's where this story begins . . .

CHAPTER 1

Room 173

The blinds were drawn to keep out the unwelcome afternoon sun as my patient lay sleeping. Her hair was dark, disheveled, and straight, spilling like ink across the starched white pillowcase. Her head slumped a bit off to the side while her glasses slid slightly off her nose. Her features were delicate. Lips thin. Her chin small and pointed. Both of her rail-thin arms were extended by her sides, IVs inserted in each bend. The previous attending nurse filled me in on this patient's condition before I took over her shift. She had just gotten out of surgery where doctors performed a laparoscopy to take biopsies from her stomach wall due to her having persistent pain. Her post-op vitals were set up and her condition was stable. Gently, I touched her cheek, willing her eyes to open. Being in the nursing profession for twenty years, being one of the first cheery voices a patient hears as the cobwebs clear when coming out of anesthesia, was a rewarding part of my career. I checked her water pitcher and smoothed her blankets, then skimmed over her patient report. She'd come around soon. All I could do was wait.

"Tricia Somers," I said softly, reading her name off her chart. It struck me because my name is Tricia Seaman—our first names are the same, spelled the same, and we share the same initials, T.S. "Well, if that's not a coincidence."

I read further down her report and spotted something right away. She was a single parent with an eight-year-old little boy and lived here in Harrisburg, Pennsylvania. My heart went out to her, being a mother myself to a ten-year-old son and three teenage girls. I was blessed to have Dan, the greatest husband and father to my children I could have ever asked for. This woman was parenting on her own. The report also noted she had no family in the area. Even more unsettling was there was no one at her bedside waiting for her to wake up. The papers went on to say she had been diagnosed with a very rare liver cancer only a few months ago. She was now back at Community General, one of Pinnacle-Health's hospitals, to determine why she continued to feel severe stomach pain after the initial reports stated the tumor was isolated to the liver.

"The poor girl," I whispered, gazing at her.

She mumbled something I couldn't decipher and rolled her head to the right. The anesthesia was wearing off. I walked over to the dry-erase board hanging next to her bed on the wall and wrote my name in big, loopy letters so she'd be able to see it easily. As I turned back around, she was fighting to hold her eyes open, watching me, sizing me up, and blinking slowly as her surroundings still blurred.

"Well, hello there," I said. "How are you doing? My name is Tricia and I'm going to be your nurse today. It's really going to be easy to remember your name because it's the same as mine and it's spelled the same way, too."

She unstuck her tongue from the roof of her mouth and groggily formed some words. "Oh . . . that's kind of neat, isn't it?" she said, gazing sleepily at the board.

I went around to the pumps at each side of her bed and checked the settings. Her side table was covered with a child's drawings and handmade crafts. That swirl of heaviness returned to my heart. So many questions trickled through my mind. So who was taking care of her child since she didn't have any local family listed on her report? I believed that all she had as a contact was a close friend. No father for the boy. No parents to rally around her. It was rare if ever I came across a patient in the oncology wing who had no one to bring him or her "Get Well" balloons. Usually there were family, friends, a circle of love around the patient. At least someone to lean on and hold their hand. This woman was like an island, alone in a sea of trouble. All I could do was say a silent prayer that her biopsies would come back normal.

I hovered nearby and let myself look at the drawings a bit longer this time. I could only imagine how hard it must be for her to be away from her son. As if reading my mind, she popped open her eyes. I'm sure she was fighting to get back to him as soon as possible.

"You can call me Trish," she said, picking right back up where our last conversation left off. "Everybody does." Her eyes struggled to focus through the glass lenses. She cleared her throat and swallowed.

> *"You can call me Trish," she said, picking right back up where our last conversation left off. "Everybody does."*

"Trish it is. That's good. So, how are you feeling?"

"I'm just trying to wake up."

"So, how did the procedure go?"

She went to nod and must have thought better of it. Too much, too soon. "Good, I think. They were able to look at everything they needed to see."

"Are you having any pain?" I adjusted her pillow a bit higher.

She closed her eyes again but stayed with me. "I'm just so tired. So, so tired."

"Well, you had a pretty big day, you know. I'm sure you need a little rest."

Slowly, she pulled her heavy lids open and focused on my face. I smiled softly knowing it probably didn't even make a dent in the turmoil she must be feeling. "I'm just hoping they can get to the bottom of what's happening," she said, taking a cleansing breath. "I need to get some answers."

I glanced back at the drawings. It wasn't my job to go any further than to monitor the patient's condition and provide the proper care. I see many patients during the day, but something pulled at my heart the moment I met Trish—maybe it was because my boy, Noah, was close to her son's age and also loved to draw pictures for me. I wanted to learn more. Something inside hungered to know her story.

I checked her IV bags and casually asked, "So, if you don't mind sharing, how did you get to this point? Can you tell me about your journey?"

I wasn't sure if I had overstepped my bounds. A sliver of silence hung between us. But then Trish opened her eyes all the way—as if the clouds had cleared and she was actually seeing me now for the first time. She pushed her glasses farther up her nose, wincing at the IV in the crook of her arm. I couldn't read the expression on her face, but if I had to, I would have thought it was desperation. She wanted to talk—that much was clear.

Trish told me she had a Bernese Mountain Dog named Molly, whom a staff member at the hospital was now dog sitting. Trish had been walking Molly every day, trying to stay fit, and eating a healthy diet. She said she felt well and even though she was dropping weight, she thought it was from all of the exercise. Then, in the fall, she began having a nagging belly pain. She tried to ignore it at first, but it only grew stronger. When she went to her family doctor, they ran some blood work, but nothing remarkable showed and the pain kept getting worse. It got to the point where even sitting upright was becoming a challenge.

"I worked in customer service, talking to customers all day on the phone, fielding problems and such," Trish explained. "The pain got so bad that I'd sit at my desk with one hand on the computer keyboard and the other bracing my stomach. I tried as long as I could to pay the rent and bills, but I had no choice but to quit working."

Trish went on to say that in October of 2013, she went to the emergency room where doctors decided to do a CAT scan, which revealed a tumor on her liver. They scheduled a biopsy. The results showed that she had a rare form of cancer, but they thought it was controlled and hadn't spread or invaded any other tissue. In fact, they didn't even think it could be the cause of all her pain. From their conclusion, this area on her liver wouldn't cause those kinds of symptoms.

"But I knew something wasn't right," she said, shaking her head. "I mean, I couldn't work. I couldn't sit up. I couldn't even stand right anymore. It's been unbearable, but I'm hoping now to finally find out what's causing it."

"Who watches your son?" I stood next to the table admiring one of his crayon drawings with a heart and the word "MOM" inside of it.

"I have a neighbor who watches him and then some trusted friends that I worked with. They take turns off and on because it's just too much to expect any one person to care for him. He kind of bounces around, I guess you could say."

I was going to suggest she must miss him, but before I formed the words, she had her phone out and was bringing up photos of him. "His name is Wesley," she said as she smiled. I noticed how much better she looked just talking about him. "He's eight years old in second grade. Look, here he is. There we are goofing around. I love his smile, don't you? I wrote him notes when I was in the hospital before. I just needed to talk to him, and he wasn't there, so I would jot down the things I was feeling. It just brings me peace even if he never sees them."

His images melted me. I could tell he was a charmer, and I enjoyed the fact she was sharing with me. It was as if she were opening the door to her heart, letting me in and holding me there. And I wanted to be there. It wasn't something I've ever felt before. Of course, I had compassion for all of my patients. I enjoyed conversing with them, trying to make them smile, and meeting their families . . . but this wasn't in that realm. What it was, I didn't know. It went beyond anything I'd ever experienced before. Yet maybe it wasn't so odd. After all, it was only human to feel sympathy. It looked like she didn't have a lot of resources and was strug-

> *It was as if she were opening the door to her heart, letting me in and holding me there. And I wanted to be there. It wasn't something I've ever felt before.*

gling on her own with her illness. It must be terrifying to lie in this bed, alone and not knowing what was going to happen. She already had a cancer diagnosis. She was in such pain and must have sensed her condition was serious. So why did I begin to feel this strong tug toward her? Why did I want to identify this feeling and give it a name?

Now that Trish was fully awake, it seemed she needed to talk, and I had all the time to listen. She told me a little about her past, her dating history, Wesley's father being out of the picture, both of her parents passed away from cancer, and she and her brother didn't communicate much. It was a heavy first conversation, especially for someone who had just come out of surgery, but Trish's words were like air rushing out of a balloon. She seemed pressured to release them. Every word spoken with such urgency. She then asked about my family, and I briefly shared about Dan and the kids. I almost felt guilty for having what she most likely ached for desperately. I also told her my parents divorced a few years ago, but that my mother lived just down the road from us in the same house I grew up in.

It had been nearly an hour and I had to move on to help my other patients. But I couldn't stop thinking of her. Wondering about her. The things she said repeated in the corners of my mind. The photos of Wesley haunted me long after I went home that night and soaked up the smiles on my own children's faces.

CHAPTER 2

The Request

After that night, I made it a point to stop and see Trish whenever I was on duty. I was no longer her attending nurse, but I wanted to be a friend to her and make sure she had everything she needed. At times, I would catch her with her coworkers and neighbors who had come to visit, and that did my heart good to see her with people who cared about her. They even seemed to know who I was—almost as if Trish had told them about me. Other times, I would find her alone, but if she'd had a visit with Wesley, she'd be wearing an ear-to-ear grin. As the days passed, she seemed more comfortable as her physical pain lessened.

After Trish had been in the hospital for three weeks, I noticed her room number lit up on the patient board signaling her discharge that day. I didn't know anything about her condition or the results of her tests. I'd been praying for her and Wesley and was eager to check on her, but my roster was full and the hospital was extra busy. It was late afternoon by the time I made it to Room 173.

I knocked on the door and poked my head in to find Trish sitting with the social worker. The cloudy April weather we were having seemed to have crept into the room and filled it with gray. There was a heaviness in the air. Something wasn't quite right. Usually, whenever Trish saw me, even if she was in pain, she'd chime, "Hey, how are you?" or "You look nice today!" But now her face was stoic as she sat in a high-backed chair next to the hospital bed. The social worker was sitting on the edge of the mattress, explaining something about providing Trish services and transportation for treatments.

"Sorry to interrupt," I stammered. "I didn't know you had anyone with you. I just saw your discharge light and wanted to come and say good-bye."

She waved me in. "No, I'm glad you're here. Come in. The tests came back."

My steps carried me forward as my mind spun with a crazy mixture of hope and fear.

"What is it? What did the doctors tell you?" I asked.

"It's not good. The cancer has spread to other areas of my body. They said I'm terminal."

The social worker sat among her forms and papers, staring first at me and then back down to her documents.

"Oh, Trish," I gasped as she rose from her chair. I walked over and hugged her. She stayed there for a second before pulling back and piercing me with her gaze. There were no tears. There was no panic. What I saw was a firm acceptance with a definite spark that there was something else about to erupt here.

"I'm glad you stopped in because I have a question to ask you."

I held on to her hand. It was cool in contrast to my clammy palms. "Okay. What is it?"

Trish took a deep breath and looked straight into my eyes. "When I die, will you and your husband raise my son?"

My knees almost buckled. I didn't know what to say. Trish was essentially a stranger. But I also felt a tugging at my heartstrings telling me to say yes. But that was crazy, wasn't it?

> *Trish took a deep breath and looked straight into my eyes. "When I die, will you and your husband raise my son?"*

Trish was waiting for my answer. "Oh, my," I finally stammered. "This is all happening very fast. You just got some terrible news, and I think it would be wise to give it time and think things through. You should consult your attorney and know your options. Don't decide anything right now. I'm flattered, but—" I struggled to find the right words for the situation but came up empty. We were strangers. She barely knew me. We met only a mere three weeks ago and even then, we've only had a handful of conversations. She didn't know what kind of house I lived in or what my family was like. She didn't know our financial situation, or if I was a lousy cook, or even if my kids were little terrors. She had no idea if my marriage was stable or any clue about

Dan as a father. How do you trust your child to a person you barely know who lives in a household of strangers? Yet, as she continued to stare while panic rushed within me, Trish seemed at peace with her unorthodox request. The social worker sat stunned on the side of the bed, silent, her jaw a bit slack, watching this moment unfold before her. I wanted to ask her what her professional opinion was but couldn't find the words. The air grew thick, and I needed to get out. I needed room to breathe.

I hugged Trish good-bye and told her she'd be in my prayers. When I left the room, I felt a sense of relief as the door closed behind me. We had never exchanged phone numbers and had no way to communicate after Trish's discharge. It was against hospital rules to look up someone's information in the medical records. Once I walked away from her, I honestly believed I would never see her again. In that moment, I sank against the hospital wall, relishing the cool feel of something solid to lean into. Slowly, I took deep breaths to calm my racing heart as I struggled to make sense of my thoughts. What just happened? As I finally got my footing and began to walk down the corridor to finish the next three hours of my shift, I realized her words followed me like a shadow I couldn't shake off. *When I die, will you and your husband raise my son?* And along with the question came an image. The two went hand in hand. An eight-year-old boy with a sweet little smile who had no idea that the only person left in his world to love and protect him was slowly fading away.

CHAPTER 3

Baby Fever

My husband's expression was unreadable. I fought to stay glued to my chair as he and I talked in hushed tones at the kitchen island. "Dan, I mean, it's unbelievable, isn't it? She doesn't even know us. How could she really want us to raise her little boy?"

The kids were upstairs, just off to bed. In the other room, a State Farm commercial was filling in for our momentary wordlessness. Someone must have left the television on.

Dan leaned back in his seat next to me, pondering, calm as always. I bit my bottom lip to keep from saying anything more. It was his turn.

"I think we just have to take this a step at a time," he said, folding his arms, weighing the matter. "From what you've told me about her having no family or other options, we can start by trying to find out what her immediate needs are like groceries, or even the ability to get her medications. Things like that."

"Of course," I answered. It was reasonable. A good next step. "That's certainly something we can do."

"Obviously, she's had a lot to take in. Just give her time to process the hard news she received today. We'll keep her in our prayers and go from there."

"Like where, exactly? Where could this go?"

I fidgeted with my hands, twirling my wedding ring on my finger. I've always searched Dan's eyes for answers. They were usually hazel, but on days when he wore blue, they'd mimic a clear summer sky. If he wore green, they'd transform into orbs of jade. His eyes were one of the first things that captivated me about him. Now, as he got lost in his thoughts, I saw beyond color. They were misty pools of compassion searching for answers and holding my reflection.

"I don't really know, Tricia," he admitted. "I think we need to trust God on this one and see what is meant to be."

> *"I think we need to trust God on this one and see what is meant to be."*

"You're talking about the adoption, I'm sensing?"

He paused and then gave a nod.

"It could be God's way of providing the right little boy that we've been waiting for from the foster care agency. Maybe the reason we weren't chosen for that last referral was because there is another child who needs us more."

I stared at the speckled countertop in front of me, holding my raw emotions in check. So much was coming back to me in waves and images. Dan and I had met years ago when we were attending the same church. I never thought of him in "that way." In fact, I actually talked more with his twin brother, David, than I did with Dan simply because David seemed more outgoing. When Dan left for college, we lost touch for a number of years. I finished high school and began college and worked toward my nursing degree. Then the summer before my senior year, I helped at church teaching Bible school. One evening I walked into the kitchen where the ladies were preparing the snacks. Many of them had known me most of my life, since pigtails and braces. They asked how I was, how college was going, and, of course, if I was dating anyone.

I groaned. "All the good Christian guys are taken," I retorted. "I'll probably end up in a convent."

I remember the ladies' hugs and reassurances that love often comes when we least expect it. I didn't quite take it to heart. I figured I'd be married to my nursing career and that would be that.

The next evening at church, I was darting up the stairway as Dan was coming down. We both literally stopped in our tracks. After a moment of recovery, we exchanged pleasantries while I tried to keep from staring. I loved how his eyes twinkled as he flashed that irresistible smile. I mean, Dan Seaman, the shy guy, was now Dan Seaman, the man—and a very handsome one at that!

He was dressed in a nice pair of shorts, a button-down casual white shirt, blond hair combed, cleanly shaven, suntanned, and smelling of musky cologne. I suddenly felt flushed and very aware of the three years since we'd spoken. Hopefully, he noticed that I'd done some growing up, too.

Our chance meeting on the stairwell led to a wonderful dating relationship. He was so easy to talk with—caring, relaxed, and genuine. I loved how his expression lit up when speaking of family and his faith in God. I never felt so comfortable with anyone before. It made it very easy to say yes when he proposed six months later on Christmas Eve 1993 under a covered bridge during a light snowfall. We married the following November (and Dan's nervousness caused him to cut his neck shaving, which left a blood spot on the collar of his white dress shirt, and later backed his car into the Dumpster at the church). Our wedding was everything we dreamed it would be, surrounded by loving family and friends. After a honeymoon in the Bahamas, we settled into a cozy apartment in Middletown, close to Harrisburg. I finished my bachelor's degree at Millersville University and Dan began his career at Highmark Blue Shield, a health insurance company. I also worked part-time at a hospital in Lancaster while I finished my classes. We loved having our own little space to call home and being near all the restaurants and shops. I quickly learned that Dan had a knack for decorating, too. Just another thing to add to the list of why I fell in love with this man.

In October of 1995, our marriage would endure its first real test. My grandmother on my father's side suddenly passed away in her early sixties. Her name was Anna, and I was devastated. We were very close, and imagining never seeing her again tore my heart apart. I leaned on Dan like never before, and he was my rock, just as I knew he would be. But the loss hit me hard, and I started longing to leave Middletown and go back home to the country. It felt like everything inside of me changed. I no longer wanted to be surrounded by buildings, traffic, and busyness. In my grief, I yearned for simplicity, being close to family and in wide-open spaces. Dan and I made the move, and it was perfect except for one thing: we were ready to start a family of our own.

Soon we were able to experience a small taste of how it would feel to be parents when we babysat my three-year-old cousin over-night one weekend, taking her to Chuck E. Cheese's and toy shopping. While I had a blast, Dan felt overwhelmed. He slumped against our sofa and raked a hand through his hair.

"I don't think I'm ready yet," he said. "I just don't know if I can do that. It was exhausting."

My mouth hung open in surprise, as I felt quite the opposite. I wanted to be a mother now more than ever. "Are you kidding? That was so fun. What part of that was exhausting?"

He eyed me cautiously. "I don't really know if I'd be good at it. I've never been around kids or even changed a diaper. Besides, I'm not sure I'm ready to share you."

Dan soon overcame his reluctance, and we were lucky to get pregnant right away. Our sweet little Anna was born on October 23, 1996. Although initially he was afraid he would break her, Dan soon got used to being a daddy and embraced every moment of it. Two years later came Jenna, born on October 27, ironically the same day my grandmother died. I always felt that was God's way of saying I needed to have joy now. He transformed a day of sadness into a celebration of new birth and life. Jenna looks just like my grandmother, which I thought was very special. Anna was named after her, but Jenna resembled her. It was as if my grandmother were all around us. We were so happy with our beautiful girls that Dan and I decided to try for another child. Baby Emma was born on August 29, 2001. Dan took a first look at her and said it was like God took Anna and Jenna, put them in a bag, and shook them all up, creating the spitting image of both of them combined. Even today, she still looks like both of her sisters. Two years later, we were elated when we discovered we were pregnant again. I gave birth to our first boy, Noah, on February 20, 2004. It was with great amazement and a touch of shock that Dan went out to the waiting room after I delivered to announce to the family, "It's time to buy some trucks! It's a boy!"

Since we had our hands full and needed my income, I worked mostly weekends so Dan could take care of the kids. During the week, I'd be home while he went to his job. It was a lot to juggle, but we couldn't have been happier. With a newborn, a one-year-old, a three-year-old, and a five-year-old, our van was filled with car seats and toys. I remember loading the kids up, packing Sippy cups, snacks, diapers, then looking at Dan with a beaming smile and exclaiming, "Wow, we've got our hands full, don't we?"

Dan turned into such a great dad after all his initial fears. He would make the kids sandwiches cut into the shape of Noah's Ark and use animal crackers on top making it fun for them to eat. He would do this every weekend when he was in charge. On Monday when I took over, the kids would moan and say my food was boring and not like Daddy's Noah's Ark. I'd firmly tell them, "I'm not making you that. I'm making you a regular sandwich." Once it became apparent that he was "Mr. Fun," I reminded him of the old days when he once thought he couldn't do this and be a good father, but now he was quite the pro. We laughed and hugged, feeling as blessed as two people could be. That is until a dark cloud formed over us stealing my happiness away.

At the time Noah was born, I had my tubes tied. It was never anything we talked about at length or something Dan forced me into. He always assured me that it was my decision. It just made sense at the time after having our fourth child, so why come back for the procedure later when I could have it done right then and there? Besides, the doctors warned me about trying to get pregnant again because after having C-sections with Anna, Emma, and Noah, I had a lot of scar tissue that would make another birth complicated. But looking back, I began to realize I wasn't emotionally capable of making a sound decision right after giving birth. As time went on, it was something that I began to agonize over. It felt like a part of me had died.

"Oh, what have I done?" I cried in the circle of my husband's arms. "I didn't make a good choice. What if we want more children?"

We looked into getting the procedure reversed, but it carried risks and was very costly. There was also no guarantee that after spending that much and going through the surgery I would be able to get pregnant. I went through a lengthy period of mourning, struggling constantly with regret until one Sunday at church, we got to talking with some friends. They had adopted a child and knew many other couples who were fostering or had adopted children. Dan and I discussed it, and we both felt hopeful. There was an answer if we ever decided to add to our family.

As we were running a busy household, juggling careers, and raising kids, the years passed quickly. Noah was eight when Dan and I felt ready to pursue an adoption actively. Since we knew several friends who had gone through the process, we realized it wouldn't be easy, but we had our hearts set on a baby boy, seeing as Noah was outnumbered by his sisters. My arms ached to hold an infant again. I missed the velvet soft skin, the little wrinkled fingers, the downy hair, the scent of baby powder and soap bubbles. I wanted a baby to cradle and cuddle. A huggable bundle to hum lullabies to. After a few starts and stops with another agency, in the spring of 2013, we contacted the Bair Foundation Child & Family Ministries and felt a strong connection with their staff. We went to their training seminars, filled out reams of paperwork, and endured home inspections. One thing that struck me about the training was that the instructors focused a lot on teaching us about grief and loss. It opened my eyes because, as we began the adoption process, all I thought about was the result: we were going to get a child! A baby! Dan and I would be new parents again. But what we really learned was the fact that, yes, that is the goal, but also that these children have to lose something in order to come to you. To me, that was profound. All I had thought about was getting a sweet little bundle, never thinking about the reason that child was available. In truth, either they had lost a parent or they'd been through severe

From that point on, it wasn't about what we wanted—it was about what God wanted.

trauma. Hearing this changed our mission. From that point on, it wasn't about what we wanted—it was about what God wanted. It was about us being prepared to minister to a child and fill a void and a need. We weren't putting in our order for a perfect little boy. We were opening our family up to be faithful and serve what God had placed on our hearts. With our new enthusiasm, we were thrilled when we were officially approved by the agency and started receiving referrals. We were so excited and thought the profiles of available baby boys would come instantly. Naïvely, I thought if the agency marked our application with the rubber stamp saying "APPROVED," our phone would start ringing off the hook. We soon learned it doesn't work that way. The real name of the game was patience.

CHAPTER 4

Where the Road Leads

The waiting was agonizing. I would find quiet time just to spend with God, praying today would be the day we received a referral. After all, God knew our hearts had room for one more, and I knew there were so many children needing a loving family. It seemed like such an obvious solution, yet weeks and weeks passed by. No phone calls. No emails. No word at all. I began to wonder why finding a baby to love was so difficult.

After two long months, just after the New Year of 2014, we got our first referral from the Bair Foundation for an adorable eighteen-month-old boy. His history stated his rights were being terminated, meaning he would be available for adoption to the right family. Along with his story, his background, and personal info, they supplied a photo that held me captive. It was a profile image—the agency's rules allowed you to see the child only from the side to protect his or her identity, but what I saw was enough to turn my heart into a puddle. He was sitting on a three-wheel

Little Tykes bike holding onto the handlebars. His hair was blondish brown. I couldn't see his eyes, but in my mind, I imagined they were brown. After examining everything they sent, we had the opportunity to submit our profile. Once submitted, there could be many other families the agency was also considering. The caseworker for the child would review them all and choose the best match based on many factors. Dan and I, along with the kids, happily answered yes to be considered.

I remember coming to terms with the referral not being the infant I had planned on. This little boy was one and a half years old. Yet when I'd pull his photo up on my computer screen, I'd blink back tears of joy. I kept enlarging the image, trying to see every bit of him, before the picture would become blurred and I'd have to size it back down. I would study his shirt, his little jeans, his laced sneakers, the little pink seashell shape of his ear. I observed the way his tiny hands gripped the handlebars of his bike. There was no shortage of adorable here. I was in love. I bubbled with excitement to prepare for this perfect little boy to join our family. I went out and bought blue crib sheets, toys, and a special little blue-and-tan stuffed puppy. I was ready. More than ready. I was a new mother waiting for her son to come home.

But after weeks went by and we got no word, I kept prompting our caseworker Sarah to see what she could find out. Email after email, she kept saying she had inquired, but wasn't getting any response. Finally, after checking my inbox for the hundredth time for an update, I saw the words I couldn't bring myself to absorb: "I honestly think they probably placed him elsewhere since we would have heard by this point. Don't give up. We'll get another referral."

For the first time in my life, I got angry with God. It didn't feel good at all. God was my rock. My hope. My only place of comfort when nothing else did the job. But what possible reason could there be to open my heart to a child who needs love in return—to open our home to a child who has none— and have it all fall through in the end? How did that make sense in any way? It didn't. In fact, it was horribly unfair. I couldn't understand His reasons or any plan that could explain why this adoption wasn't working. All

> *For the first time in my life, I got angry with God. It didn't feel good at all. God was my rock. My hope. My only place of comfort when nothing else did the job.*

I knew was that my heart felt raw, as if it had been sliced with a blade and I was slowly bleeding. The pain was so great, I nearly decided to give up. The waiting and risk of losing another referral were too much. Thankfully, good friends encouraged Dan and me to keep trying. They told us that it wasn't unusual for this to happen and that the child God intended for us was out there somewhere. I remember hugging the stuffed puppy I bought for the baby against my wanting heart and venting my agony toward heaven.

"I don't understand You, God," I cried out in prayer. "Where in the world is my baby? I've got to believe what I keep feeling deep inside. You know our most passionate desire. You also know the needs of the little boy You've chosen for us so he'll have a happy home. Please, I beg of You, bring us together! I'm hurting. Where is my baby?"

The moment after I released that prayer, an instant wash of calm flowed over my body. My rapid breathing slowed, the anger died like roaring flames to an ember. It was then I felt God's presence and heard His distinct whisper. *Trust in Me. Wait upon My timing. Your son will soon be home.*

After discussing Trish's request with my husband, I sat at our kitchen island, leaning my head on Dan's shoulder. That prayer of loss I sent up to the heavens that day now came back to me like an echo. Could it be that God hadn't turned a deaf ear but already had the perfect son chosen? Not a baby. Not a toddler. Not even a referral, as we had been praying for. But an eight-year-old boy who had no one to care for him but his mother. A mother who just found out her son would have to send his love from this earth up to heaven one day soon.

"So what do you think?" my husband asked. "Taking this one step at a time with God's help seems pretty logical."

"But what do we tell her? What if she asks again and we can't give her the answer she's needing? I don't want to make anything harder for her than it already is."

"Tell her the truth. That we are there to help, and whatever is meant to be will be."

It didn't make sense to me. Trish's life was ticking away like a stopwatch, and we were going to tell her that we'd simply see how things went when it came to the future of her son? It felt like telling a drowning victim that we'll maybe throw her a life raft. That there are no answers now, but we'll just have to wait it out while the current keeps pulling them deeper. How could I look Trish in the eyes with that kind of approach?

I'm not a patient person, and that often made situations harder. There were so many times while I was waiting for hope and direction from the adoption agency when I thought I'd fall apart. When our one and only referral fell through the cracks, I longed for God's reasons but couldn't hear His voice. I made demands. Like a child throwing a temper tantrum, I wanted Him to make sense of it all right now. When I finally stopped forcing the issue and remembered whom I was battling, I knew where I could find His instant answers. I would curl up on the sofa with my Bible, skimming Scripture. God wasn't absent, He was so beautifully near. In the midst of all of my efforts to control things, I had somehow forgotten. Yet, while scouring the pages, there was one passage that especially spoke to my pain. I read Proverbs 3:5 (NKJV) over and over:

"Trust in the Lord with all your heart, and lean not on your own understanding." It applied then and it surely applied now. His Word was the only thing that made sense. I knew I had to cling to it if I was going to make it through, no matter how challenging blind faith can be.

I paused as the unanswered questions and anxiety still nagged at the corners of my mind. "I think you're right," I finally said. "We'll reach out to Trish and Wesley and help with whatever they need. We'll trust God to lead us from there. I can make peace with that."

I planted a kiss on Dan's cheek and relished his arms wrapping around me. What I didn't say was that God was pulling us in a totally new direction with a plan that surely wasn't one with ours. Yes, I knew we were to trust in the Lord and not try to figure out the future by ourselves, but it was scary, to be honest. None of this was something I expected. To go from planning for a baby from an adoption agency to considering a boy in elementary school who literally came out of nowhere caught me completely off guard. I was Trish's nurse for a short time in the hospital. What made her believe with such certainty that we'd be a good fit? Wasn't there anyone else she could consider? We were two strangers. It was all so emotional and complicated, yet I felt strangely aligned with something I didn't quite understand. Underneath all of the uncertainty was a sense that God was at work in His way and in His timing. I closed my eyes and kept replaying the prayers I cried out to Him for so many months. To send us the right child. To fulfill this constant yearning. To complete our family with a little boy who needed us as much as we needed him. My visions of crib sheets and lullabies gave way to placing my heart in God's hands. For the first time since coming home that day from the hospital, I smiled.

CHAPTER 5

Beyond the Hill

N ow that I had a plan, I wasn't sure how to execute it. I had no contact information for Trish, yet I couldn't wait at least to hear her voice again. It had been two days since she was discharged and already she'd been consuming my thoughts. Did she have groceries? How was she managing to take care of Wesley? Was she in pain? Was anyone looking after her at all? Then it came to me. I remembered a four-legged, tail-wagging, massive Bernese Mountain Dog named Molly. The dog sitter Trish had told me about, Robbin Babb, would be the one with her contact information, and she conveniently worked at PinnacleHealth.

Robbin was a physical therapist, and although I didn't know her very well, I had seen her before. We had spoken about patients, but never anything on a personal level. Once I tracked her down, I touched a hand to my short brunette hair, trying to look as casual as possible, while on the inside, my anxiety level was off the Richter scale.

"Hey, Robbin," I said, my voice an octave higher than normal. "I understand that you're helping out with Trish Somers's dog."

She stared back at me, a bit perplexed. Most likely, nobody on staff knew anything about the dog sitting and even if they did, the likelihood of it being the center of conversation was nil. Her dark eyebrows furrowed together in confusion.

"Yeah, actually I am," she answered. "How did you know that?"

"It's kind of a long story. Do you have a few minutes to talk?"

We needed a private area free from the hectic hallway traffic, so she followed on my heels to a nearby medication room. Once we got there, I took a moment to gather my thoughts. As I politely smiled at her, I couldn't help but wonder how in the world she took Molly for her walks. Robbin's a tiny bit of a thing, as big around as my pinky, with eyes the color of melted chocolate, and she wears her brown hair pulled back in a smooth ponytail. I pictured Robbin going through the neighborhood with this 110-pound gigantic breed of dog on a leash barreling ahead of her like a locomotive yanking the poor girl behind.

"So, how did you know I was taking care of Molly?" Robbin asked, cutting through my visual.

"Trish told me. I was her nurse when she came out of surgery, and it came up in conversation along with a lot of other things."

She blinked, still bewildered. "I'm not sure I follow."

I told Robbin the story of taking care of Trish that first night, the conversation we had, and how I had popped into her room to check on her during the next few weeks. When it came time to explain what happened between us the day of her release, a fist knotted in my stomach.

"She asked me something right after she told me that she was terminal," I said, still unable to truly comprehend my own words. "She asked if my husband and I would raise her son when she dies. That's exactly what she said to me."

The orbs of Robbin's deep brown eyes grew wide. "What? Oh, wow. That's quite a request, especially when you barely know each other!"

"Yeah." I nodded with a nervous laugh. "Well, it's all I've thought about since that day. I can't explain it, but I'm not running scared. In fact,

> *"She asked me something right after she told me that she was terminal," I said, still unable to truly comprehend my own words. "She asked if my husband and I would raise her son when she dies."*

my husband and I have discussed it, and we both agree it feels like God is up to something here. The problem is I never got her contact information. Would you mind giving it to me?"

Robbin rubbed her arms. "I've got goose bumps! That's really amazing. I've got both her cell phone numbers, her email, and I've been to her apartment, so I know where she lives."

She went on to explain that she met Trish in the fall when she was in the hospital for her initial symptoms. Robbin worked with her as a patient then, putting her through various physical exercises to help her to gain strength back. During one of their conversations, Trish told her about Molly the dog, who was the size of a bear and a true handful to care for. Apparently, her neighbor was less than enthused to volunteer for the job during Trish's stay at the hospital. According to Trish, Molly could be rather stubborn and had a habit of setting down her very large rear end and refusing to move until she's good and ready. It was quite challenging to try to argue with an animal you couldn't pick up, push, or drag.

"As it turned out, my husband and I recently lost our dog, and I was missing those doggie kisses," Robbin explained. "Plus, my heart just went out to her. I ended up giving Trish my cell number and telling her if she ever needed a pet sitter not to hesitate to reach out to me. That's exactly what she did a few weeks back when she was admitted again for the lap procedure. Trish said things were getting worse, so I stepped in and took Molly to our place, where she's been staying ever since."

A beat of silence fell between us. It was clear that Robbin cared for Trish, too. We shared that common thread and somehow just knowing that gave me a sense of much-needed hope.

"What should we do?" I asked.

"I really think we ought to make a visit. I've been trying to keep in touch with her to see how she and Wesley are doing. Let's both go down and spend some time with them. Maybe we could get them some things from the store. It's got to be hard for her to get out and about. We'll see how things go from there."

We made a pact. Robbin was all in. I now had a partner with whom to move forward.

We planned to meet at Walmart a few days later after Robbin got off work to pick up some things Trish and Wesley might need. I got there first, and since it was the middle of April, I found myself wandering up and down the Easter aisle putting together a basket for Wesley. Trish was certainly in no condition to do anything like that herself, and I couldn't imagine him going without. I chose a yellow basket that looked like a chick and filled it with all kinds of candy and little surprises like sidewalk chalk and bubbles. Then Robbin found me, and we went on to purchase some groceries and paper goods. I had called Trish, who said all she could eat were popsicles, so we stocked up on those, too. She'd also asked for an Easter egg coloring kit, so we added that to the stash. Trish seemed so pleased we had connected again—and I certainly was, too. So happy, in fact, that I immediately put a card in the mail letting her know I felt badly about my reaction before her release. I wrote a note apologizing and explaining that I was taken aback initially but also told her that my husband and I agreed we'd be there for her and wanted to help as much as we could. I hoped it would brighten her day now that she was back home and on her own. It still wasn't clear what would happen regarding her request about Wesley, but I was anxious for her to know someone cared and that she was no longer alone.

"My hands are shaking, Robbin," I said as we were checking out. "I'm nervous to see her again and to meet Wesley."

"It's going to be fine, Tricia," she assured me. "I think there's a reason for everything. You watch. This whole thing will just fall right into place."

I followed Robbin to Trish's address. We pulled into an apartment complex where there were four buildings altogether, each having three units and a small blacktop area for parking. I scanned the rundown property as my skin prickled with unease, gathering my things from the car and making doubly sure to lock my door.

"Where is Trish's apartment?" I asked.

She pointed off in a downward motion. "There. Just watch your step."

There was a little stone walkway with a rickety railing that went down a hill. How in the world had Trish made this treacherous climb in her weak condition? As we descended the hill, straight ahead I could see a Dumpster. To the left was her apartment door with a small concrete front porch. My breath snagged in my chest as Robbin knocked twice. This was the first time Trish and I would see each other since she asked me to raise Wesley. Had she changed her mind now that she had time to think more clearly? Did she regret ever asking? Did she decide on a coworker or friend to whom she'd rather entrust her boy? That would make sense, of course, but when I dared to stretch my thoughts even further, I realized that if she hadn't changed her mind and everything was still the same, I could be meeting my son for the first time today. What would I say? This isn't how I pictured it happening! I had blue crib sheets still in the package, for Pete's sakes! And what would

Had she changed her mind now that she had time to think more clearly? Did she regret ever asking?

he think? Surely, he had no idea about his mother's request or the importance of this visit. Of course, he knew Robbin from caring for their dog. To him, I was just some lady tagging along. And then the door opened.

"Oh, hi," Trish greeted. She seemed excited to see us. "Wesley, we have visitors and there's someone I want you to meet."

She was dressed in an oversized pajama shirt, stretch pants, and fuzzy pink slippers. Her hair was pulled back with loose strands spilling down as if she had been resting. The chemo she had just started was obviously taking a toll, as she moved gingerly and looked a bit pale. Still, she appeared so much happier and relaxed in her own environment.

I glanced over Trish's shoulder to where Wesley was sitting on a kitchen chair, wearing headphones and focused on his Nintendo. When he slid them off and stood, he was taller than I imagined he would be. And he didn't walk the short distance to the doorway—he sort of hopped and jumped. He grinned, showing me his small, square teeth, his brown eyes bright and shining. He wore jeans and a tee shirt that looked a couple of sizes too small, and he had chestnut hair that stuck up here and there in short, wayward spikes. He seemed to have springs in his feet as he bounced behind his mother while looking at me as he waved. I felt my mouth go dry as I smiled and gave a little wave back.

"You know Robbin, but this is Miss Tricia who took care of Mommy when she was in the hospital this last time," Trish told him.

I stared a bit too long, cleared my throat, and tried to loosen my rigid posture. Once I was able to move and force myself to act somewhat normally, I edged forward and touched him on the shoulder.

"Hello, Wesley," I said, keeping my tone steady. "I've heard so much about you. I put together this Easter basket hoping you might like it. I've got a son close to your age, and he just loves jelly beans and those little marshmallow chicks."

"Wow, thanks!" he said, tearing into the candy just as an eight-year-old would, unwrapping the little chocolate bunnies and shoving piece after piece in his mouth until both cheeks bulged.

I could tell right away that Wesley was a special boy. I had met him only a few seconds ago, but already I was lost in watching him. He sifted through the basket for just the right color of jelly bean, examining several until he found a red one and devoured it. I studied how he chewed, how he sort of hummed to himself, how he kicked his feet back and forth. He continued to move constantly, to stay in motion every second, even when simply sitting.

"Well, come in, come in," Trish insisted, stepping aside.

There wasn't much daylight coming in the small window, making it necessary for a small lamp to be on despite it being a sunny afternoon. We maneuvered our way toward the kitchen to put the groceries away but had to be cautious where we stepped because of the clutter.

"This was so great of you," Trish said, taking things out of the bags and putting them away.

"Can I help to wash those dishes?" Robbin offered, gesturing toward the stack of plates and bowls in the sink. "I know you need your rest and I'd like to help."

"No need," Trish answered, placing a bottle of apple juice in the fridge. "We can manage."

But just as Trish spoke, Robbin opened the door of the dishwasher, which had no room for dishes at all. Instead, it was being used as a storage spot. Inside were random containers, folders, pads of paper, and notebooks. I turned away, but was then met with a baker's rack piled high with school papers. Next to it was a little desk with pencil boxes and crafting items. I wondered if that's where Wesley sat to draw those precious pictures for his mother's hospital table.

The three of us ladies then settled on the couch while Wesley darted back and forth between the living room and his room. It occurred to me that the candy I'd supplied was fueling his already over-the-top energy levels. I hoped Trish didn't mind. If she did, she didn't say so. Wesley seemed used to doing things his way, and Trish's illness probably left him to fend for himself quite a bit. I sank back against the cushion and spotted a dusty VHS cabinet in the corner of the room. On top were a handful of "Get Well" cards with the one I sent her in the middle.

She saw where I was looking and gave a soft smile. "It meant the world to me to get your card," she said. "I'm glad you and Dan didn't think I was crazy asking you what I did that day."

I wasn't prepared for us to approach the topic so soon. I expected a prelude of chitchat. My pulse drummed in my ears as I observed her sudden, uneasy smile. All I could do was wonder where this conversation was leading and give a nervous smile in return.

CHAPTER 6

What's Left Behind

So there it was. The invitation to talk about the question I had replayed over and over again in my mind. She was probably about to laugh at herself and ask me to erase the whole thing. She didn't mean a word. It was, indeed, just her panic speaking as she grappled with what the doctors had told her. Forget it. Move on. I glanced over at Wesley, still bouncing around and eating the head off a marshmallow Peep, finally settling into a chair in the corner with his headphones on playing his Game Boy. I would only have this conversation if he was completely out of earshot.

"We never thought you were crazy at all," I assured her. "My husband and I talked at length and what we certainly agree on is that you are a mother who deeply loves her son."

"You are a mother who deeply loves her son."

Her gaze searched and found him. I watched her melt with adoration. "Yes, I do. Very much. He's my everything."

"Do you mind my asking more about Wesley's father?" I pushed on. "In the hospital you mentioned he wasn't in the picture, but I'm not clear on the circumstances."

Trish shared her story. She was born and raised in Pasadena, Maryland, and had an older brother named Ollie who was married to a lovely lady named Erin. Trish enjoyed a close relationship with her parents, Oliver and Sylvia, and lived in their home until her early thirties. She worked various jobs and loved hanging out with her coworkers and friends, especially her best friend, Maria. They were quite the pair—working all day and partying all night, waking up the next morning to do it all over again. The lifestyle was fun, but Trish longed to have a place to call her own. On the meager wages she earned, she needed as much patience as time to save. When she turned thirty-two, she was finally able to buy herself a town house and was so proud to move out and gain her independence. But this new phase of life didn't last very long. Soon she learned that her mother had been diagnosed with cancer. Trish rearranged her work schedule and made sure she was always available to take her to doctor appointments and treatments and to be a support for her worried father. Just when things seemed to be looking up and her mother's condition improved, her father was also diagnosed with cancer. It seemed unimaginable, as if the bottom were dropping out from her world. Concerned for her mother and wanting to help with her father's care, Trish barely spent time at her own place. It only made sense to sell her town house and move back home where she was needed. Her father's cancer was aggressive, and he soon succumbed to his disease. Just as she was grappling to come to terms with that loss, her mother's cancer returned and progressed past the point of no return. She died a short time later, almost as if life without her husband wasn't an option. Her brother, Ollie, had been faithful in helping Trish take care of their parents and always made sure Trish knew he was there for support. When both their father and mother reached the end stages of their lives and had to be hospitalized, Ollie would make the trips back and forth to be with them until their final breaths. Trish stayed back at the house, unable to cope with seeing them hooked up to tubes and machines, watching them fade, smelling death in the air. She confessed she still carried that sense of shame but hoped that despite her absence in their final days, her parents knew how very much she loved them. Lonely and lost, Trish continued living in her parents' house, wrapping their memories around her like a warm blanket. She was alone now. Her brother returned to his life. Now it was up to her to piece together one of her own.

"I guess at that point all I thought about was finding someone to love," Trish explained. "That's when I met Ben [not his real name] on a dating site, but he was bad news. Had my father been alive, I can promise you, Ben would have never gotten through the front door."

Ben moved in with Trish after going out together a few times.

He was tall, poured on the charm, made her laugh, and was someone to lean on, but it didn't take long for her to grow disillusioned with the relationship; there were more arguments than cuddles. Ben never held down a job for very long and wasted no time spending most of Trish's inheritance. He drank a lot and had a hot temper. Trish's friends and her brother urged her to break things off, yet she wouldn't listen to them. She knew Ben best. All relationships had hurdles, and she was determined to work things out. But when the drinking and violence snowballed as months went by, she finally had to draw the line and admit everyone was right. She and Ben were toxic together. She kicked him out and planned never to look back.

Shortly after the breakup, Trish realized her period was late and discovered she was pregnant. It wasn't anything planned. It surely wasn't something Trish knew how to handle. It was tempting to keep it to herself and not share the news with Ben, but something nagged at her to tell the truth. As turbulent as their relationship had been, this child was his, too. She decided she had no right to keep such a secret. For a short time, she believed this unborn child was the miracle their broken relationship needed. Ben moved back in, took Trish to her obstetrician appointments, and even held a steady job. Her friends and brother were far from happy, but Trish had renewed hope. With the baby and Ben, she would finally have the family she always wanted. She'd have two people to love.

On November 29, 2005, Wesley was born after a long and difficult labor resulting in doctors performing an emergency C-section. That moment was golden in Trish's memory. It erased all the pain and fear. All that mattered was this new life was here safe and sound. With Ben by her side, she beamed as the doctor cut the cord and held the infant up for her to see, wailing with his little fists clenched, a crown of dark brown hair matted to his head. Only after Trish's passing would I learn that she kept a journal filled with notes she wrote to Wesley knowing one day he'd be ready to read them. Out of all of her entries, those about her pregnancy and the birth of her son were the most passionate and detailed. On the page where she expresses her joy after his birth, she tells Wesley in crooked handwriting:

I fell in love! You were the most perfect thing I had ever seen!

Ben and Trish brought their new baby home. Parenthood did not improve their relationship, however, and things quickly began to deteriorate. With the baby crying at all hours of the night, Ben grew agitated since he had to rise early for work, and he would snap at Trish to keep things quiet. To avoid any conflict that could easily spark an argument, Trish would gather Wesley in her arms and sleep in another room where she could cuddle him, feed him, and hum lullabies sweet and low, to make sure her son stayed silent and calm. Sleeping together was something they continued to do even now that Wesley was in second grade, Trish admitted. They never learned to face the dark of night on their own. The two were inseparable—they felt safe by each other's side. As long as they had the other nearby, all was right with the world.

> *The two were inseparable—they felt safe by each other's side. As long as they had the other nearby, all was right with the world.*

When Wesley was just short of a year old, Ben and Trish got married. She loved weddings and wanted to do it up in grand style complete with finding the perfect dress, a lovely, long white gown that made her feel like a princess. The music, flowers, and small gathering of guests distracted her from the underlying current of disapproval from friends and her unhappiness in the relationship. Maybe if she just kept going through the motions, things would magically turn into the life she always imagined.

Despite wanting the happily ever after and the kind of love her parents had, Trish eventually realized she had to end her relationship with Ben. They were divorced by the time Wesley was four years old. Trish had taken Ben's wrath before, always waiting it out and accepting empty apologies, but things were different now. She had a reason to stand stronger. There was an incentive to draw the line. The son she loved above all else was entitled to better childhood memories. How would he ever learn what real love was if all he ever heard was fighting, screaming, and glass breaking as empty beer bottles were hurled? Once the papers were signed and she was finally free of Ben, she concentrated on the only blessing he had left her. No matter what it took, she vowed to give the little boy who owned her heart the future he deserved.

Determined to have a fresh start, she sold her parents' house and moved to Pennsylvania. The job market was better there and monthly expenses could be cut if they downsized to an apartment. Many of the ones she applied for wouldn't accommodate Molly the dog, so Trish ended up in Harrisburg in the tiny dwelling I was sitting in that day. She always meant to fix it up or look for someplace better, but then she got sick, and the rest is history. This would have to be home.

I could tell Trish was tiring from the visit and filling me in on her past. We had been there for nearly two hours. Robbin and I both said we should be leaving, as we didn't want to interrupt their dinner. I glanced about and wondered where they sat to eat a meal together. There was no dining room table to be found.

"You're not interrupting anything," Trish said. "When we get hungry, we just get something out of the refrigerator and throw it in the microwave."

It jarred me a bit to think that was what dinner meant to them. In fact, it tore at me much deeper than I was prepared for. I still didn't know this woman well and I especially didn't know her little boy. But I had a strong feeling inside that God was pulling me closer, leading me to do something. What exactly, I didn't know. Was I to be Wesley's mom as Trish had asked? Or was I just someone to cheer her up during her last weeks as a caring friend? Maybe I was simply the lady who took care of Mommy in the hospital. The lady with the Easter basket filled with goodies. Someone who sent a card in the mail. I grew dizzy with more questions than answers. Dan said to leave it up to God, and I had agreed, but in that moment, I wished I had a direct line to heaven on speed dial to figure this all out! What was my role in this family's life?

> *But I had a strong feeling inside that God was pulling me closer, leading me to do something.*

Robbin and I hugged Trish and said good-bye to Wesley, then headed up the stairway. When I got to my car, I embraced Robbin and thanked her for coming with me. And then I started the journey home. Yet, as the apartments faded from my rearview mirror and an hour later the rolling green countryside of McAlisterville soothed my soul, I wished I could share this piece of paradise with Trish and her son. After spending time together that afternoon, I was changed forever. There was no getting around it. I could pull into my driveway, greet my beautiful husband and children, make a dinner of chicken and biscuits, then watch the sunset from the rocker on the front porch, but not all of me would be there. Not like it was before because—ready or not—once I left that itty-bitty apartment, a part of me stayed behind.

CHAPTER 7

The Easter Visit

Easter was just a few days away and was always a special occasion for Dan and me. We would start the day by gathering the kids and meeting the rest of my family at the morning church service. From there we'd head to my mom's, where we'd enjoy a family dinner with all the trimmings and then end the day with an Easter egg hunt in her yard. It was one of my favorite holidays, but this year I couldn't get into the spirit without thinking of Trish and Wesley. Would sharing our tradition and celebration with them be a gift or a burden? Something told me they'd enjoy it. But perhaps they might already have some plans. Maybe her friends from Baltimore who visited her in the hospital were making the trip to come see her. Trish told me about Maria, who was like a sister to her, and how dear all the girls were to her heart. Wouldn't she rather spend Easter with them? Or maybe she and Wesley had a little family celebration planned. I had no idea what their holidays were like but hoped Trish would at least consider the invitation. I checked with

Robbin to see what she thought of the idea, and she was all for it. In fact, Trish recently mentioned to her that she and Wesley would most likely just heat up a piece of ham. That was the extent of it. Not only would it be a great break for Trish and Wesley to get out and have a real Easter dinner but it would be the first time my family would meet the two of them and we could see how Wesley might fit in if he did eventually come to live with us.

Since sharing with Dan about the apartment visit, we both knew things were progressing beyond our initial intention of helping with small things like groceries. After what I saw—knowing how the two of them lived—I could barely concentrate on much else. There was a connection that I couldn't explain and the sense that God was blending our families into one. It was just a sensation I had deep inside, and Dan could feel it, too. We decided it was time to have a family meeting. We couldn't keep moving forward toward the possibility of adding Wesley to our family without knowing how the kids felt about it. So, as we gathered them around the table, I folded my hands in my lap and was greatly relieved when Dan took the initiative to give this conversation a nice introduction.

> *"She's met someone special at the hospital . . . one of her patients. She needs help, and we feel God drawing us closer. But if we do this, it will include all of you."*

"Your mom and I have something to discuss with you," he said to the group. "She's met someone special at the hospital . . . one of her patients. She needs help, and we feel God drawing us closer. But if we do this, it will include all of you."

Emma, along with the rest of them, widened her eyes. "What kind of help?" she asked.

That was when Dan set his gaze on me. There was my cue. "Actually, her name is Trish Somers and she has terminal liver cancer," I explained. "She's a single mother with an eight-year-old son. She asked if we'd raise him in our family when she dies. We're really considering it."

I always knew we had some beautiful children who carried God within their hearts, but when I saw them nodding in approval without hesitation, it brought me instantly to tears.

Noah nodded enthusiastically. "I'd have a brother close to my age that I could actually play with."

Dan and I smiled. "You weren't too into the changing-diaper idea, were you, buddy?" Dan asked.

"Baseball is a lot more fun and doesn't stink, either." Noah shrugged and giggled.

"It's so sad," Anna chimed in. "I can't imagine what his mom is going through. Of course we should help. I'm all for it."

"How long does she have?" Jenna's expression clouded with compassion.

I hesitated. I'd never said it out loud before. It was harder than I thought. "The doctors expect six months at best. Her cancer is aggressive despite the chemo she is going through."

A silence hung among us as the kids digested that thought. It was a lot to take in.

Noah raised his hand as if he were in class. "Can we meet them? I want to play with—"

Dan laughed. "Wesley. His name is Wesley, and we've decided to invite them over to spend Easter with us. They don't have family, so this will be nice. We'll all have a chance to get to know one another."

There was one more component of the situation left unsaid. I knew it had to be made crystal clear. "Wesley has no idea his mother is dying or that she's asked us to raise him when she's gone," I explained. "Don't say anything to him about any of this. All he knows is that we're new friends here to help them and have fun with."

Heads bobbed. "No worries, Mom," Emma replied, speaking for all of them. "We'll be careful about not letting anything slip. We'll just be nice to them and get acquainted."

> *Our entire family was on the same page. God had us all in the palm of His hand.*

I sat back, relaxing for the first time since we all gathered. "If we're in agreement, then I think it's a good time to pray."

Without further discussion, Dan led a prayer for guidance. As he asked God to direct our path and reveal His will to us, I could feel such a beautiful unity. Our entire family was on the same page. God had us all in the palm of His hand.

The next step was to call my mother, my brother, our pastor, and several close members of our church family. The more we shared about Trish and Wesley, the warmer and more welcoming everyone seemed. I was stunned—this wasn't exactly the route we planned for adding a son to our family, but against all odds, the pieces seemed to fit. Our hearts had room for one more, and we wanted a brother for Noah. Trish had no one to raise Wesley when her time on Earth was done. We had a home that wanted a little boy, and Trish had a little boy who needed a home to put her heart at peace. It meant letting go of the dream I had to add a little baby to the household. The stuffed puppy, the blue crib sheets, the paperwork at Bair saying we wanted an infant—well, it seemed a logical enough goal to aim for. But beyond the countless prayers Dan and I said together asking God to help us be patient while He chooses the right son, I couldn't deny this certainty I felt about Wesley. So he didn't need a crib or diapers or lullabies. His needs went far beyond that. I reflected back to the grief training we went through at the foundation that now seemed so fitting. It taught us about children who lose their parents. Little ones who have endured trauma and heartache and loneliness. We learned that the child we would be accepting into our family would be there because they had lost so much and had absolutely no one to love them or care for them in this world. My eyes misted as I thought of precious Wesley, who didn't know what was waiting ahead. He knew his mommy was sick, but he surely didn't know this illness was a battle she couldn't conquer. In time, he would have to be told. He was an intelligent little boy—very observant. He would surely notice Trish losing more hair, wasting away, unable to eat, too tired even to smile at him. The two that slept together since he was a baby would soon be torn apart.

The Bair training was supposed to prepare potential foster or adopting parents for a hurting child who would be joining their family dynamic. But now I saw it through clearer eyes. The veil had been lifted. I began to see that God hadn't put us through the special training for the baby I'd cradle in my arms . . . just maybe He was preparing us for a very special eight-year-old who would soon lose the only family he'd ever known. It wouldn't be easy. I certainly knew that. The transition would be very difficult for everyone on so many levels. Wesley wouldn't only be grieving the loss of his mother; he'd be thrust into a new family, different surroundings, and a new school. He'd go from being used to entertaining himself to being surrounded by three sisters, a brother, and a new set of parents. In a blink of an eye, this child would have an instant family and a whole new future. Then I had to consider our side. Although I was thrilled Dan and the kids were open to this, I still had some reservations. From what I observed on my first meeting with Wesley, he was a high-energy kid, while Noah was a mellow little soul. Would they get along? Wesley was also very independent and kept to himself, while we were very close-knit and used to doing lots of things together. Furthermore, we had rules and boundaries set in place for our children, while Trish let Wesley do as he pleased. I knew she was too weak physically to parent as she wanted to, so he was left to fend for himself, grabbing snacks on the run and probably even going to bed at whatever time he felt like. This could be like mixing oil and water for all we knew, but underneath all the "what ifs" and somewhere in the center of my jumbo tangle of fears, God kept whispering, *Trust in Me and be anxious for nothing. Follow where I lead.*

> **God kept whispering, Trust in Me and be anxious for nothing. Follow where I lead.**

That evening I made the call to Trish and asked if she and Wesley would like to join our family for Easter. I was so excited when she agreed. In fact, she said she couldn't think of anything she'd love to do more.

The plan was for Robbin to drive Trish and Wesley halfway between Harrisburg and our place so Dan and I would have to make only a thirty-minute trip to pick them up after church. The kids would go home from church with my mom to her house where the festivities were being held. We'd meet them there later, along with my brother, Adam, my sister-in-law, Jessica, and their kids, Parker, Owen, and Addison. There'd be wonderful food, loads of playmates for Wesley, and wide-open spaces where Trish could sit and enjoy the fresh country air. I hoped we'd get the chance at the day's end to stop by our house so Trish and Wesley could see our home. I was so excited that I had to remind myself to breathe.

Dan and I met Robbin at the gas station we'd agreed on. Dan connected with both Trish and Wesley instantly. Trish gave him a welcoming hug, and I could tell she liked how he helped with her things. The second Dan mentioned he was a Legos fan, Wesley's face brightened. But I held back a bit, concerned about some changes in Trish since our last visit. She had gotten her hair cut short because the chemo was causing it to fall out. That was expected, but it was difficult to see just the same. She was dressed in capris, and I quickly observed that her legs were starting to swell. She moved slower and was more unsteady on her feet, most likely due to the medication she was taking with the chemo. It was a red flag that certainly caught my attention. All I could do was pray this day wouldn't be a mistake.

CHAPTER 8

Trial Run

When we pulled into my mother's driveway, my family—the whole lot of them—ran with anticipation toward our van. Noah's face lit up. He was like a kid on Christmas morning! Dan and I got out, and then we helped Trish to her feet. We then waited for Wesley to hop out with his usual energy, but instead he stayed back. The kids craned their necks to see through the window to try and catch a glimpse of him, but he retreated and refused to come out. I did a quick head count and realized this poor child was being bombarded by seven children all at once who were surrounding the vehicle ready to play with him. They had no idea that Wesley's world consisted of his Lego table and a Game Boy, not playmates with loud voices and giggles. Only when he saw that my sister-in-law brought real live baby bunnies with her for the kids to enjoy did he dare to climb out. Then he broke into a smile, petting the soft fur and watching their noses twitch.

The kids played while the adults got dinner on the table. Trish sat nearby chatting about how lovely my mother's home was and how much she enjoyed the banter of a big family. It was something she never had and always wanted. My mother complimented her on what a beautiful son she had raised. Those words meant a lot to Trish, and I could see a glow of pride light up in her eyes. Of all that went wrong in her turbulent life, Wesley was the one thing that was perfectly right. Then we called all the kids to the table and after a prayer, we all dove in. The food was abundant and delicious. My mom served a baked ham, mashed potatoes, corn, gravy, and a crisp green salad. Trish fixed a plate for herself and kept saying how good it smelled and looked, but after a few bites, she couldn't manage any more.

"I think my eyes were bigger than my stomach," she offered as an excuse. "Perhaps I can eat something later."

Wesley, on the other hand, snacked on chips, took a few bites of ham, and chugged down a full glass of soda. He had no interest in anything else on the table.

As the day went on, I grew worried about Trish's condition. After our meal, I wanted to take her to a place away from all the activity and get some fresh air. I got her a chair and we sat in the sun. I made sure she had a glass of water. She enjoyed the warmth of the rays and kicking her sandals off to put her bare feet in the grass. She even got to hold the baby bunnies and nuzzle them to her face.

"They are so adorable," she drawled, her speech a bit slurred. "Look at their noses go up and down."

Every so often, an alarm would go off. Trish had a few cell phones she kept with her at all times set to let her know when to take more medication. Whenever I'd hear that beeping, I tried to figure out how much time had passed. How closely was she taking these pills? Her unsteady movements, slowed and slurred speech, lack of appetite, and swelling in her legs signaled to me that she was taking too much. The more doses she took, the groggier she became—not at all like when I saw her before. As more meds got into her system, she blinked slowly, seemed tired, and didn't flash as many smiles. The chemo was definitely wearing on her even though she hadn't been on it long at all. Shortly after she left the hospital, her doctors started treatment, trying to buy her as much time as possible, but with that borrowed time came a price. She suffered side effects like losing her shiny dark hair and having her electrolyte balance thrown off. She lost her appetite and was struggling physically, but despite it all she kept thanking us and saying how they were enjoying their day.

At one point, Trish excused herself to go inside and use the bathroom. I jumped up to hold onto her—she seemed so weak and unsteady. As we headed toward the house, she caught her foot on one of the pavers in front of my mom's porch and fell forward and scraped her leg. Dan rushed out, and we both got her into a lawn chair. He kept an eye on her while I dashed inside and got the first aid kit to clean her bloody shin.

"I feel so bad," I said, dabbing and fussing. "That shouldn't have happened. I thought I had a hold of you."

"It's not your fault," she said, still woozy with pupils dilated.

"Does it hurt?"

"Nope. I'm fine."

"Are you sure?"

"I'm sure."

I shrank back a bit and smiled. "Do you want to give that trip to the bathroom a second try?"

She leaned on me and stood. "My bladder and I would, thank you."

"I'm really sorry I'm being such a nurse. I guess it's just my instincts."

She grasped my arm as we took slow steps back toward the house. "I don't mind. To be honest, it's nice to be taken care of."

As the afternoon went on, the kids enjoyed an elaborate egg hunt, which was great except for one thing. Noah came to me frustrated at one point, and I feared the worst: what if Noah and Wesley were incompatible? But it turned out that Wesley was playing with my nephew instead of with Noah. Parker was eight, the same age as Wesley, and the two seemed like two peas in a pod already.

"I've waited all these years for a brother and today he comes and he doesn't want to play with me," Noah cried. "All he wants to do is play with Parker!" I couldn't help but smile. I pulled him close and wrapped my arms around him. It was hard to explain, especially when he'd imagined Wesley was like a UPS package with his name on it—a brother to run, laugh, and play with, delivered right to the doorstep. But there were a few snags that were a bit heavy for a small child to understand. I grappled for a way to help this rather unusual situation make a bit more sense to him.

"You've got to remember, Wesley has no idea he could one day be your brother," I said, keeping my voice safe and low. "He knows his mommy is sick and we're going to be helping them, but we haven't explained to him that we could be his family. So, for now, just be patient, okay?"

He pouted his lip and stared at the kids, especially as Wesley ran circles around Parker. "Okay," he finally groaned, wiggling from my embrace. "I just want him to like me."

I dotted his nose. "He's going to love you. Just give it a chance."

Reluctant to see the day end, we invited Trish and Wesley over to see our house. Despite Trish being fatigued and wobbly, she agreed, her energy somehow renewed. When we all piled out of our van, Noah and Wesley raced about the yard, finally beginning to bond after the little hitch earlier. I worried as we walked around our place, watching Trish's expression and Wesley's reaction. I wanted them to like it. I knew it was silly. I knew there was nothing not to love about our house nestled in the beauty of the countryside, but I was imagining it through Trish's eyes. This could be the home she sent Wesley to when she passed. It had to be perfect. Every room. Every piece of furniture. Every throw pillow, wall hanging, and scented candle. Even the piano where Anna played the most beautiful songs and hymns. It all had to pass inspection with flying colors. I wanted it not to be just a nice place for them to tour. I wanted them to feel the love. To know this was home. To show Trish that this was where Wesley's future could unfold.

I wanted them to feel the love. To know this was home. To show Trish that this was where Wesley's future could unfold.

"Does everything look okay to you?" I asked Trish as she leaned on me and carefully made her way from the kitchen to the living room. "Is the house okay? Did you see all the room outside for the kids to play? Do you like it?"

Trish looked into my eyes with an expression of sheer contentment. "Oh, it's perfect," she sighed. "It's beautiful here. It's just what I pictured it would be."

"Good. So good. I'm glad that you like it and you feel comfortable."

She smiled just then, that sparkle I'd noticed in the hospital just weeks before flickering back in her eyes. "It feels right. I'd live here if I could!"

After a glorious day, Noah and Emma decided to accompany me on the drive back to the gas station where we'd be meeting with

Robbin to drop off Trish and Wesley. As soon as we arrived and began gathering things out of the car, Wesley ran to a row of bushes and retched, vomiting and holding his stomach. Trish immediately tended to him, rubbing his back and waiting until he was finished. She walked him back to Robbin's car, where he got in, and then she joined me as I stood stiff with worry.

"Oh, my goodness," I said. "What do you think it is?"

"I have no idea. He usually doesn't get sick like that. I can't remember the last time he threw up."

We exchanged good-byes and Robbin's vehicle pulled out of the parking lot. I said a prayer as I watched the taillights fade down the road. My nursing instincts told me Wesley wasn't suffering from a virus or overeating. I wondered if Wesley knew in some deep part of him what was happening. Did he know today wasn't just an Easter fun day? In his gut, was he aching and hurting already for the darkness looming ahead? Did he have some idea that all the fanfare and playmates and the grand house tour were leading up to something? In my heart of hearts, I sensed this little boy was a lot more intuitive than we gave him credit for.

CHAPTER 9

The Waiting Game

After our first trial run as a family, Dan and I knew it was time to get things on paper. The first meeting went incredibly well. Wesley was so cute and really warmed up to the kids, who absolutely adored him. But Trish was losing ground, and that meant taking things to a whole new level. We had all grown attached—it felt very personal. The question of whether or not we'd raise Wesley was now not a question at all in my heart. So the next step was for us to be named his guardians if things with Trish took a turn for the worse. We were an approved foster family, but there was no guarantee the dots would be connected if something were to happen. Everyone at the hospital knew that if Trish hit bottom and needed to be admitted and it got to the point where the social worker was called, they should make sure the Bair Foundation was alerted. The foundation knew now what was going on as well. If a referral came through for Wesley to be placed, we'd be in the system and considered. Still, without formal paperwork outlining Trish's directives regarding whom she wanted to raise her son, Wesley might not end up with us. Trish agreed and told us she had actually gotten some things in writing. We found her an attorney, but she didn't follow through. She kept saying she had so much going on but she'd be sure to get to it. It left me unsettled because when the doctors gave her the grim diagnosis, they expected her to have six months to a year before the cancer would claim her. Should I pressure her with all she had on her plate? I'd already fallen in love with Wesley. I had a special bond with his mother. If we lost him now and he went to total strangers, I didn't know how I'd cope. Especially when I knew Trish was so sure about us being the right family for her beloved son.

"We just have to trust that if God intended for this, it will all work out," Dan said. Somehow, he didn't feel the hurricane of emotions I did. Instead, he was at complete peace with it all. Thank God, opposites attract.

> *"We just have to trust that if God intended for this, it will all work out," Dan said.*

After Easter, either Robbin or I would check in with Trish every day. Robbin went over to the apartment after work to bring groceries and make sure Wesley was doing okay. I would call or text just to show Trish she was on my mind. The weekend after Easter, Trish's friends came to visit her from Baltimore. Maria and the girls would be staying all day Saturday before heading back home. When I didn't hear from Trish Saturday night, I figured she might have been tired from having visitors, but when Monday rolled around and neither Robbin nor I could get hold of her, a panic began to brew. It was the first time Trish fell off the radar, and it made me feel very uneasy.

Finally, on Tuesday afternoon Robbin and I got word from the hospital that Trish had been admitted. The American Cancer Society volunteer came to her apartment late Monday, April 28, to pick up Trish for treatment. When he knocked on the door, Wesley answered. He had a toy in hand and had been playing, but the volunteer looked beyond him and saw Trish lying on the couch incoherent. When Wesley explained that his mommy had been sleeping "for a long time," the volunteer called 911. With all the commotion, a neighbor came over and took Wesley back to her apartment as Trish was transported. Wesley had stayed with the neighbor before, so he went calmly and willingly. When I looked at the timeline, it seemed unfathomable. After Trish's friends left Saturday night, she never responded to calls or texts. She was found and admitted to the hospital late Monday afternoon. I would later learn from Wesley that he simply thought his mommy was tired and sleeping. He played and when he got hungry, he knew how to work the microwave, so he made himself something to eat. I wasn't even sure where or if he slept. At one point, he said he thought his mother was hungry, so he got a banana and tried to feed her, but when she didn't move, he figured she was still just sleeping. After doing the calculations, it seemed Trish was unconscious, leaving Wesley on his own, for two days. What if she had died and we still didn't have any paperwork in place? The boy would not only lose the only mother he'd ever known, but he'd also be lost in the system.

Not knowing what to expect, I rushed to start my shift the next day and went directly to Trish's room. I was terrified. If she was so far gone that my face didn't ring a bell, what would happen? Wesley would most definitely go into a foster home. Trish's plan would be ignored. I knew with my entire heart that she wanted her son to be raised in my family. Dan and the kids knew. Our church knew. My mom, my brother, Robbin, the hospital staff, and Trish's girlfriends knew, but nothing was in place to make it happen legally. As I approached her bedside, I saw her gaunt and asleep with IVs in her arm to hydrate her. Within seconds her eyes fluttered. She was starting to come around. I gulped as her gaze widened and focused directly on me. There was no smile. No sign at all. I held my breath as I reached out and lightly touched her face.

"Do you know who I am?" The question hung in the air along with the sterile aroma.

She answered right away. "You're Tricia."

I gasped and nodded. "Yes! Thank you, God! I'm so glad that you remember. What in the world happened?"

She seemed confused and said she really didn't know. As her thoughts became clearer, she tightly grabbed my arm. "Am I dying?" she asked, her head coming off the pillow. "Am I dying right now?"

"No, no . . . I don't think so. I think you're very dehydrated from the chemo."

She settled down a bit and licked her dry lips. "We still have so much to do."

Wesley. She was talking about Wesley, but where in the world was he? When I asked, she wasn't sure, but she thought he was probably with the neighbor. After she made a call to verify he was indeed there, a bit of the turmoil was settled. Throughout the day, she became stronger and more coherent. As glad as I was to see that, I knew I still had a very important phone call to make. One that couldn't wait.

Pastor Arthur Mott is a gentle giant standing over six feet tall. He and his lovely wife, Joyce, have been like family to us for the last sixteen years and are the very soul of our home church. When my kids were little, they couldn't say "pastor," so they called him T. Mott and it stuck. He always had the best hugs that could soothe all my cares away and a heart the size of the state of Pennsylvania.

So when I called him and he picked up on the third ring, I couldn't contain my words.

"T. Mott . . . I need you."

That was all it took. He told me he'd be right there and before I knew it, he arrived at the hospital. He already knew about Trish and all that had been going on with us. The church had been praying for us steadily. When I filled him in on the events of the last few days, he asked about her faith.

I had never heard Trish mention her religious beliefs. I even tried to think if when I sneezed she said, "God bless you." There wasn't anything in my memory to point to her having a faith.

"I don't think she's religious," was all I could answer.

"Well, first things first," he said.

He went into her room and spent a good amount of time with Trish alone, speaking privately, just the two of them. To this day, I don't know what exactly was said. I didn't feel it was my place to intrude on such a personal moment, but what he did tell me once he came out was that Trish had accepted the Lord into her heart on that first day of May. He had asked her if she knew where she was going after she left this earth. She replied she did not. Trish shared that she believed there was a God, but didn't really know Him. She also had doubts that God could forgive her for her past sins and failures. She wasn't proud of things she'd done. She tried to be the best mother to Wesley but felt at this point that if she was really going to get through this, the two of them needed to get closer to God.

I believe it was at this time that Trish wrote Wesley another note. It is on a bright yellow piece of paper tucked inside her journal. I still well with tears when I read it as I see this as a real breakthrough for the two of them and the source of strength that Trish turned to in order to face the long road ahead. She didn't share the letter with Wesley, and at that point, he still didn't know her fate. But I believe Trish was imagining that one day he would have the journal and read all the words she stored up to say to him:

I love you very much! I'm sorry that I may not be here to see you grow up! It doesn't seem fair, does it? You may be very angry or sad, but please understand that if we trust God and follow the path that He has given us, He will walk through it with us so that we can handle anything. God loves us, so we are to love Him and everything should be all right. We haven't gone to church or read a Bible together, so it is hard to figure it all out sometimes. Things happen for a reason. I promise that we will not only say our prayers at night, but we will go to a church to get to know God better. You must know that He loves you and will continue to love you when I'm gone. Things will be okay. You are strong. I love you!

Once Trish was released from the hospital it became imperative a situation like this never happened again. Because the American Cancer Society volunteer found Wesley alone and unattended when he discovered Trish, the county's child welfare service, Children and Youth, got involved. While they didn't file charges, they warned that we had to put a system in place so that Wesley would never be endangered again and so that we could reach Trish's friends and neighbor if we could not reach her.

But then, another problem presented itself. Trish's legs began to fill up with fluid and became badly swollen. It made it very difficult for her to care for herself, let alone take care of Wesley, too. I wanted to observe her and see if perhaps her meds needed adjusting, or worse—have her assessed to see if it was a sign that the cancer was progressing. That wasn't something any of us was prepared for. Not this soon. Trish and I had become a part of each other in an odd sort of way. We were drawn together so powerfully. There were so many memories I hoped and prayed we could make together. She needed to be with Wesley, to share his smiles and be his mommy a little longer. She needed a chance to experience how it feels to have people who love and care for her. But time had to be on our side. There had to be more sand in the hourglass. Echoing in my heart were the words Trish said to me earlier: "We still have so much to do."

> *There were so many memories I hoped and prayed we could make together. She needed to be with Wesley, to share his smiles and be his mommy a little longer.*

CHAPTER 10

A Day to Remember

Mother's Day was coming up, and Dan and I didn't want Trish and Wesley to be alone, especially with Trish's legs getting so swollen and uncomfortable. So we asked if they might like to stay with us overnight that weekend. To my delight, Trish agreed.

So on Saturday, I drove down to the apartment. Trish's legs were so bloated that even getting her up the hill into the car was nearly impossible. She struggled just to take each step. When I asked how she'd been getting Wesley to school, she answered matter-of-factly that she was driving him there as she always did. I glanced back at the unstable railing, the hill, the rusty old Dumpster and marveled at her determination. The elementary school was only a block away, but Trish didn't want him walking alone and always drove him without fail. She shared that she would start early in the morning, since it took her nearly half an hour to climb up the hill. She would crank up the car, drop Wesley at his school, come back home, and take her meds. She then set her alarm so she wouldn't sleep through and could return in time to pick him up. According to Trish, no one at school even knew about her being sick. Not even Wesley's teachers, which she was adamant about. I wasn't sure if it was because she wanted him to blend in with the other kids and not have a "situation" or if she feared anyone knowing would poke their nose into their home life and possibly take her son away and place him in the foster care system. I was in awe of this woman fighting against the odds to love, protect, and raise her little boy even if it took her last breath.

Back at our house, Dan and I set up chairs outside so we could watch the kids play. It was hard for Trish to get around, so she mostly enjoyed the rocker on the front porch. Her lips would curve into a delicious grin, just breathing in the open air, scanning the mountains on the distant horizon, and most of all hearing Wesley's laughter as he chased after Noah. Even the girls enjoyed hanging with Wesley as they chatted and got lost in fits of laughter. You would never know they weren't all natural siblings. As we watched them, I knew Trish and I were both thinking that very same thought.

"Are you excited about the photographer coming tomorrow?" I asked, breaking the silence. "It will be really special for you and Wesley to have some nice photos to always remember this Mother's Day by."

I chose my words carefully. It took all I had not to let the tears roll down my cheeks. But Trish was proud. She was strong and so utterly stubborn and independent. She wouldn't want me to go into the real reason for these photos. She knew as well as I did the cold, hard truth. That at this time next year when Mother's Day rolled around again, Wesley wouldn't be able to snuggle in her arms, smile for photos, and give her gifts, a card, or even a hug. That this day from now on would be a day of only memories.

"I can't wait," she beamed. "What a special treat. Do you think Jenna will help with my wigs, since she's so good with hair? I brought a few so we can find one that looks the most like my normal hair used to."

"I'm sure she'd love to. You'll be beautiful."

"Oh, and maybe I can get a vote on my outfit. I brought some different ones, but I'm not sure what to wear. I want to look my best."

The woman never failed to amaze me. Here she was, so swollen from the waist down that she couldn't move without being wheeled about or carried, yet she packed for this weekend like a starlet going to the red carpet—wigs, outfits, and all.

I patted her arm, overwhelmed with emotion. "You're going to be breathtaking. These photos will be absolutely perfect. Everything you want them to be."

Trish pulled her focus from the kids in the yard over to me. "Thanks, friend," was all she said, knowing I fully understood what was unspoken.

On Sunday morning, we went to church. Since Trish's talk with

Pastor Mott at the hospital, I knew she and Wesley talked more about God and even said their prayers together, but this was Wesley's first time in a Sunday service. He was excited and found it challenging to sit still. Trish loved the music and seemed completely serene. Her newfound faith gave her more rest in her soul than ever before. Afterward, Pastor Mott and Joyce greeted them warmly. It was a wonderful chance for Trish and Wesley to meet face to face with so many of our good friends and church family who had been holding them in their prayers. But, as excited as I was to share in the service, I was distracted and concerned by the continuous swelling in her legs. She was barely mobile at this point. I kept thinking, *How is she doing this?* We would walk very short distances before she had to sit and rest. Thankfully, one of the church members rounded up a wheelchair to loan to us for the day. Trish was relieved and settled into it with a sigh, happy not to have to put pressure on her legs any longer.

Once we got back to our house, we had a special lunch. We'd eaten together before, but this meal was different. It brought such joy to see our families joined back together. With it being such a glorious, sunny day, we decided to eat out on the deck. Dan grilled steaks while I prepared creamy potato casserole, green beans, and my homemade apple cobbler. I was quickly learning that while Wesley was a picky eater, he'd chow down any meat as long as it was drowned in a pool of barbecue sauce. Trish still picked and only nibbled at her food, but she did comment that it was the best steak she ever had. Once I gave my mother her gift and my kids gave me theirs, Trish surprised me with a neatly wrapped present. She knew I loved birds and had gotten me a beautiful solar light encased in treelike branches with two birds sitting on top of it. It was an outdoor decoration meant for a garden, but I couldn't let it out of my sight. I told Trish I would always keep it inside because I never wanted it to get ruined. I hugged her long and tried my best not to give in and cry. Then Wesley handed me a gift bag. I looked into his little round dark eyes as he gave a shy slip of a smile. I whispered a "thank you" and dove into the colored tissue paper, where I found a lovely bronze metal bird wind chime. It made a soothing sound in the warm breeze. I was completely bowled over by their thoughtfulness and equally amazed that Trish could even muster the energy to get to the store to purchase these kindhearted gifts, let alone afford them. But if there was anything I had learned over the short time we'd been friends, it was that when Trish set her mind on something or cared for someone, nothing could match her determination.

If there was anything I had learned over the short time we'd been friends, it was that when Trish set her mind on something or cared for someone, nothing could match her determination.

Later that afternoon when the photographer came, Trish took charge and orchestrated every photo. Of her three outfits, she chose a long floral skirt with a fuchsia top. The girls had all helped to select and style her dark, short wig, the shade that most resembled her natural hair color. Her makeup was simple, including a soft pink gloss on her lips. I had never seen her look more beautiful. She'd point out a blossoming tree, and I'd follow her lead, pushing her in the wheelchair to the exact spot where she wanted to pose with Wesley and then with my family and me. She made it crystal clear that no way, no how was that wheelchair going to be a part of these pictures, so we'd lift her under the arms and position her where she wanted to stand. I watched her keep fussing over Wesley to make sure he stayed clean, constantly fixing his hair. Trish looked simply radiant that day, although she was much thinner now and her energy was on empty. But once Wesley cuddled against her and they smiled widely for the camera, I could see an aura of pure joy radiated around her. All that mattered to her was her son. He was her very heart and soul walking around on the outside of her body. Nothing in the world brought her more happiness than simply loving him and having him near.

> *All that mattered to her was her son. He was her very heart and soul walking around on the outside of her body. Nothing in the world brought her more happiness than simply loving him and having him near.*

Looking back on it now, I know that as we teamed up to tend

to Trish, and voices and laughter filled our home, it felt more and more natural. It seemed our family was stretching and expanding. Trish and Wesley weren't guests. We weren't people here to help them and do a good deed. I truly felt in the core of my being that we were a circle of love that God brought together. Maybe not in a perfect way. Not without a cost. The grim certainty of the future hung over us like an unwelcome canopy, but somehow our togetherness was able to outshine it. How many days we had left couldn't compare to the ones we were sharing. Ever so slowly, we were building memories as a new family. And the thing about memories is that they go on forever. Nothing, not even death, can ever steal them away. By the time I had to drive Trish and Wesley back home, I already missed them before they even got into the car.

"Mom . . . wait a second," Anna said, catching up to me in the house as I was grabbing my purse. "You know, this Mother's Day was like none other. Most mothers and their children spend the day with their mom, giving them flowers or special gifts. But today I watched you with a lady with cancer, driving her around our yard in a wheelchair and picking her up. You spent the entire day doing for someone else. This is probably the most special Mother's Day you've ever had."

I swiped her long golden hair with my finger. Her tender insight touched me beyond measure and filled me with pride. "It really was," I said, tears welling in my eyes. "It was because I got to share it with Trish and Wesley, as well as all of you. I will never forget this amazing day."

Noah came along when I drove them back that night. As we helped bring their things back and forth into the apartment, Trish took it very slow and steady down the little hill, gripping the banister. On one of my trips back up to the car, I heard Wesley whooping with excitement.

"Hey, Noah! Take a look over here!" he shouted from the apartment's Dumpster. "I think I see something!"

I immediately grew uneasy, not wanting either of the boys to hang around down there. But, boys being boys, it was an adventure.

"Be careful," I called after them.

Just as Trish and I finally got inside, we heard a commotion coming right behind us.

"Look, Mommy!" Wesley exclaimed, puffing up as proud as could be. "Look what I found for your legs!"

He had lugged up an old square stool from the garbage. Like the man of the house, he dragged it over and set it right in front of the couch where Trish sat.

He helped put her legs up and then stood back. Noah and Wesley watched with anticipation as Trish let out a sigh of ecstasy as if she were sinking into memory foam pillows at a five-star hotel.

"Ahhhh, that feels better," she said with contentment.

Wesley was the happiest that I had ever seen him, hopping up and down, thrilled to have found the diamond in the rough in the Dumpster on Mother's Day. Who was I to question it? In fact, once I shook off my germophobic thoughts, I saw a loving little boy taking care of his sick mother.

I got Trish something to drink. She was clearly exhausted and it was time to head for home. The last time I did so was with an urgency to get out of the cluttered apartment and back into open spaces with room to move and air to breathe, but not tonight. Not after a weekend that proved what I already knew. We had become a part of one another. Two mothers who met such a short time ago had somehow become woven together like a mismatched tapestry with love as the thread, creating something unexpected and remarkable.

"I don't want to leave you here," I blurted out—even catching myself off guard by my words.

She stared, perhaps in surprise. "I don't want you to leave me here."

The boys ran out of Wesley's room, reminding me this is how it was for now. I told her to keep her phone right next to her and offered to help Wesley into his Pjs, but in classic Trish style, she stubbornly waved the idea off.

"No need," she said. "We'll be okay. He knows what to do."

We prepared to go, and as I leaned down to hug her, Trish held on a bit longer than I expected. "This was the most wonderful day. One of the best I ever had." She whispered her words against my ear, her breath soft and warm.

"It was for me, too," I said as I drew back. It was then I had to force myself to walk out the door.

CHAPTER 11

Home, Sweet Home

As soon as Noah and I got back on the road, I got on the phone with Robbin. I explained how I had just spent the entire weekend with Trish and Wesley and shared my concern about the condition of Trish's legs. I knew her oncologist, Dr. Lily Shah, would need to be contacted right away and that Trish was most likely not going to be the one to do it.

"She's retaining so much fluid she can hardly walk," I said. "She's so swollen, all the way up to her hips. She really needs Dr. Shah to do an evaluation. I'm sure she wasn't this way the last time she saw her."

Robbin agreed, "We'll talk to Trish and see if we can't somehow get clearance to speak directly to her doctor."

"I just know something bad is going to happen if she doesn't get seen right away."

"Don't worry," Robbin said, trying to soothe, her tone purposefully chipper. "We'll team up and make sure she gets checked out."

The next day when I got to work, Robbin and I called Trish together. I asked her to contact her doctor's office and have both Robbin and me added to her HIPAA privacy papers as contact persons. She agreed, which instantly relieved my mind.

"How are your legs doing?" I asked, already knowing the answer.

"I can barely move them. They hurt and are so heavy."

"Well, Robbin and I talked, and we really want to get in touch with your doctor. It might be the adjustment to your meds, so they need to know what's going on."

Trish took the steps to add us as contacts right away, and soon I could make the call and talk to one of her nurses. I filled her in on Trish's condition, who I was, as well as the process we were going through. She told me that Dr. Shah would like Trish to come into the hospital again.

I scrambled and found someone to cover the rest of my shift, since I was supposed to work until seven thirty that night. Right after Robbin got off work, we drove down to the apartment. Trish seemed excited, since she thought it was a friendly visit, but I wasted no time and quickly set things straight.

"We talked to your doctor's office today, and Dr. Shah thinks you need to go back to the hospital and see what is going on with your legs," I explained.

She pulled back. "I don't want to do that."

Robbin placed both hands on Trish's shoulders and gave her a stern stare. "You can't go on like this, can you? You know it's the right thing to do."

"We won't take no for an answer," I added. "You've got to take care of this."

Like a worn-down soldier surrendering to captors, Trish looked at us both and waved the white flag. We worked it out where I would stay at the apartment with Wesley and Robbin would take Trish to the hospital. We weren't sure what to expect or whether they would admit her. My job now was to keep Wesley safe and happy.

Being alone with him for the first time felt peculiar. Not in a negative way, but in a kind of strange and unfamiliar way. I wanted to learn more about him. Up until now, he'd mostly played with the kids. This was a chance to see how we got along and if he'd feel comfortable with me.

I helped him with his homework and then took him to a McDonald's inside of Walmart for dinner. He seemed fine with it being just the two of us. Better than I expected. He'd stay close and nod when I asked if he was hungry and enjoyed that he could pick where we sat. He wanted a chicken nugget Happy Meal with apples and a Sprite. I ordered the chicken sandwich and fries. He chose a booth toward the back, and we settled across from each other. He wasted no time diving into his bag for the Happy Meal toy and then squeezing packets of ketchup in red globs on his french fries.

"Do you like McDonald's?" I took a bite of my sandwich, hoping that simple question would open the door to a conversation.

He nodded, his hands constantly working the little race car that came with his meal. It seemed that was the big hit. Chitchat wasn't really his thing.

"We go a lot," he said, taking a nugget and dipping it in sauce, popping the whole thing in his mouth and then running the toy car across the table.

"You and your mom? You go to McDonald's a lot?"

"Every Friday night. That's what we always do . . . did."

A mother ran by trying to catch hold of her rambunctious toddler. I gave her a quick glance as she rolled her eyes and carried the little girl back to their table. "Tell me about it. Was it a special night out for the two of you?"

"Yeah. We went to the other McDonald's. The big one where they have that play place. It was cool because they had free wi-fi so we'd bring our iPads and stuff."

"That must have been fun."

He kept his focus on the car and really never looked directly at me. "We stayed for hours and hours. Sometimes I'd play with kids there. Mom got to know a lot of the people that came there all the time, too."

I sipped my drink and imagined the scene. The two of them having a mommy and son date night, eating, meeting people, enjoying their Fridays like a holiday at the end of each week. I wanted to learn more. I wanted him to show me their world through his eyes. I knew it hadn't been easy whatsoever, but I could see he really held on to the good times.

"How are you in school? Do you like sports?"

The little toy car was now in the palm of his hand as he spun the small black tires round and round, crunching on an apple wedge. "School's okay, but I don't like sports."

"Then what kinds of things do you like to do?"

"I was in Cub Scouts, but then Mom said it was too much money, and then we had to move again anyway."

That was when the shine in his eyes slightly faded. My hand almost reached out for his, but instead I took another sip from my straw. This whole night was a lot for him. First, his mother having to go back to the hospital and now a woman he doesn't know very well takes him out for fast food and puts him through an interrogation. My instincts told me to lighten up. I couldn't cram everything I wanted to learn about this boy into one sitting.

"Hey, what do you say since we're at Walmart anyway that we go and browse the Lego aisle? You can pick out any set you want as long as we keep it at ten dollars or less."

You would have thought in that instant he'd been jabbed with a pin. He sprung up, pushed the toy car in his jeans pocket, shoved his half-eaten dinner back in the bag, and within a second was bouncing, wide-eyed and ready to go. Apparently, "Legos" was the magic word.

Once we got back to the apartment, Robbin called to tell me that Trish was being admitted. She also informed me that Trish asked if I'd take Wesley home with me.

"What about school tomorrow?" I asked.

"Let's not worry about that right now," Robbin answered. "Trish just wants to know he's safe."

As soon as I hung up the phone, I found a plastic bag and began to hunt for some of his clothes since I had no idea how long I'd have him. I explained to Wesley what was going on, and he packed up some of his toys and favorite stuffed animals, filling his backpack and zipping it up. Obviously, he was used to having his life uprooted on a moment's notice. I suggested he also bring some schoolwork, since I thought we could at least see that he didn't fall too far behind. From there, we drove to the hospital, where Trish could see Wesley and I could give the apartment keys to Robbin. After a sweet good night to his mom, Wesley and I began the drive to my house. He sat in the back, playing and keeping himself busy. I gripped the steering wheel, then stole glances in the rearview mirror as I began to feel panicked. My chest grew tight as my lungs refused air. A rambling dialogue ran through my brain. *Who does this? Who in the world does this? I have a little boy in the back of my car with a plastic bag filled with clothes. We have no idea what's going to happen to Trish, and I'm driving him to my house!*

"When are we going to be there?" Wesley interrupted my racing thoughts.

"Pretty soon," I called back over my shoulder.

Less than three minutes later . . . "Are we there yet?"

"Almost."

"What's taking so long? How come there are no streetlights out here?"

"We're in the country. We don't have streetlights."

He groaned and squirmed against his seat belt. "It seems soooooooooo long!"

Wesley's needs put my momentary hysteria in check. What mattered was this child's well-being. I distracted him with alphabet games and a spur-of-the-moment story about an otter until we finally pulled into our driveway. He grabbed his backpack and bounded out the door as soon as the engine stopped. I could barely keep up with him. This child was a constant whirl of motion. I glanced at the stars twinkling above and wanted to ask God if He really thought I could handle this. I reminded myself to take a cleansing breath instead. God makes no mistakes.

Inside, everyone greeted Wesley. He seemed more comfortable knowing the kids and the layout of the house. It was late so I retrieved an air mattress for him. Since I knew he still slept with his mother, I put it near our bed and told him if he needed anything, I'd be right there and all he had to do was call my name. I tucked him in and read a bedtime story as his eyes grew heavy. Once he fell asleep, tangled in his blanket, his little chest rising and falling, I perched on the side of our bed just watching him. So much was still uncertain.

That week our family rallied together to make sure Wesley was happy and comfortable. While I did my shifts at the hospital, Dan held down the fort and worked from

> *That week our family rallied together to make sure Wesley was happy and comfortable.*

his home office. Wesley played with Noah and the girls as he got accustomed to life at the Seamans'. I even took Wesley to our hairdresser, Mandy, for a haircut. We also went to visit his mom midweek. Dr. Margaret Hallahan, a dear friend of mine and Trish's inpatient doctor, still hadn't determined if Trish's legs were swelling as a result of the chemo or if the cancer had progressed and she was dying.

"I need to know the truth," I told Dr. Hallahan in the hallway as Wesley showed his mom his new Happy Meal toy. "What is going on with Trish? What is your honest opinion?"

She leaned against the wall and expelled a sigh, her usual bubbly personality deflated. "Tricia, she very well could be reaching the end stages."

I felt punched in the gut. None of us was ready to let her go. She'd become such a gift in our lives. It always felt like we had more time. Who would tell Wesley? How could his little heart survive such a loss? How in the world could we get all of our plans and paperwork pulled together now? What if she died before we had the chance to put her wishes on paper and make our taking Wesley into our family legal? I swallowed back my anxiety and grief, then matched Margaret's deep breath.

"If there was ever a time to believe in God's miracles, it's right now," I said, walking back into Trish's room determined to be strong for my friend and her son.

A day later, I got a call from Margaret delivering more grim news.

"Tricia, she can't go back home like this. The fluid is unbelievable. We're doing everything we can, but the scans aren't looking good. We need to get a plan in place, since she won't be able to function like this independently. We'll have to start looking for a facility for her. I'd like to call Arlene."

I knew what that meant. Trish was indeed going to have her meds evaluated. Dr. Arlene Bobonich is an inpatient palliative care doctor with PinnacleHealth and was very instrumental in taking care of Trish's symptoms, controlling her pain and nausea, as well as addressing her side effects from the chemo along with her emotional and spiritual well-being. Her input would be key in finding the best approach to adjusting Trish's medication to alleviate her suffering. Arlene was the best of the best, a tall, mature woman with gorgeous silver hair. She always made quite an entrance in her bright floral outfits with a matching handbag and shoes. So many times she'd light up the room as she practically floated into the oncology unit calling out, "Hello, dears," greeting all of the nurses. I felt a sense of relief knowing that Margaret was going to contact her and both of these wonderful women would be rallying around us to take care of Trish.

The following day Arlene called. I was surprised because I knew she was hundreds of miles away on vacation, but it was great timing since I was home and could tell her the whole story without Wesley anywhere nearby. He still had no idea about the severity of his mother's illness or that she was dying. We knew the time would come for him to learn the truth, but I prayed that time wasn't now.

"Oh, Tricia," she said, compassion softening her voice. "My dear, just tell me how I can help."

"I don't know what to do, Arlene. Things are happening so fast and Trish is freaking out because she doesn't want to go to a facility and leave Wesley."

After a thoughtful pause, Arlene laid out a plan. "We must focus on controlling her symptoms. In her weakened condition, if things don't turn around, she may have a month at best. When I get back to Harrisburg tomorrow, let's you, Trish, Dr. Hallahan, and I sit down and talk together."

I agreed and we hung up, but I was breathless with all that was happening. *Please, Lord . . . give us the time we need. Help Trish to hang on so all the pieces can fit together.* I didn't know how all of this was going to go down, but knew I had to talk to Dan right away. That night the two of us once again sat around the kitchen island where this whole journey began.

"We can't let this happen," I said, battling tears of frustration. "We need more time and to get things put in writing. And where is she going? She's terrified, Dan. She'll be miserable in a facility away from Wesley."

My husband studied my face, cupped my hands inside of his, warm and steady, my forever-safe haven. "Honey, I don't know how we can look at Wesley with a clear conscience and tell him we want him but not his mother. If he's truly going to live here and we are serious about raising him, then we have to do right by her and care for her and love her just as we would any member of this family."

Of course, he was right. His discernment floored me. I sagged with relief, threw my arms around him, and hugged him with all of my might. "I love you, Daniel Seaman," I said. "You're amazing. I don't know what I would do without you. This would never be possible without your support."

We pulled apart and he told me he loved me, too. Then he gave a sheepish grin to lighten the mood. "And you said I was the one who brought my work home with me."

I dabbed my tears, as we both broke into a fit of laughter that felt like a good rain after a very long drought.

The next morning, Trish called. I could barely understand her words through her chokes and sobs. "I can't believe this is happening. Can you keep looking after Wesley? I don't know where they're going to put me, but I can't bear the thought of being away from him."

"Trish," I said calmly.

"I'm so broken. I've never been without my son."

"Trish," I repeated, "have you checked your text messages today?"

Her sniffling stopped. My question must have felt like a shoe on the wrong foot, very clumsy and out of place. "Well, no, I haven't. I've been too upset with all this going on."

"You check your messages and call me right back."

We hung up and I waited. I pictured her in the hospital bed scrolling her phone and finding the text I sent her just before her call. I worded it from my heart and smiled as I imagined her reading it. It said: Would you like to come live with us? Would you like to be our family?

I counted twelve seconds before my cell phone chirped and I placed it against my ear. I didn't have to say hello. Trish did all the talking and it was one word over and over. "Yes! Yes! Yes!"

CHAPTER 12

A New Direction

The next morning Dr. Shah and I spoke at length about Trish's condition and what it would mean for us to bring her to our home. We would need help in getting her a special hospital bed, a list of all her medications and when she should take them, home nurses and hospice workers to come by the house when needed, and transportation for her doctor appointments if Dan or I wasn't available. The road ahead was going to get rocky, but somehow I felt sure we could do it. God doesn't give us more than we can handle. I had to trust Him on this one.

It was also important to speak with Trish with complete and utter honesty. The aggressive chemo wasn't working and was probably why her legs were swelling. She wasn't responding well to it, so it was time to change her medication and aim to control her symptoms, but I had no idea how she would take the news.

Trish was in her bed sipping water when Dr. Shah and I came in. I couldn't get over how thin she was getting. The ridge of her collarbone protruded sharply above the neckline of her hospital gown.

"Am I getting discharged today?" She sat farther up and adjusted her pillow.

I sat next to her and cupped her small hand in mine. "We need to talk first," I said. "Before you come home with us we need to have a plan laid out so you can feel better."

Dr. Shah stepped a bit closer holding Trish's patient report. "The key at this point is to try to slow the cancer down and to control your symptoms," she explained. "The cancer can't be cured, but we can change the type of chemo medication you've been taking so you can be more comfortable."

Trish looked defeated, as if hearing she was terminal for the first time. "Just slow it, but not beat it. I guess I was still hoping for some kind of miracle."

> *I looked at this woman who had gone from my patient to a dear friend.*

I looked at this woman who had gone from my patient to a dear friend. I no longer monitored her vitals, checked her IVs, or kept her water pitcher full. Now I had to try to be the wall she could lean on. I had to be her strength when she got dealt a blow. I slid closer just to let her feel my body heat, but wanted so badly to embrace her completely.

"We're all here for you," I uttered, wishing I had words more powerful. "You won't have to face things alone."

She looked down and laced her fingers together, a tear slipping down her cheek. "I don't want to give up on killing the cancer. I was hoping the chemo would work. I wanted to keep fighting."

"And we want you to fight," I said firmly. "But fight for making more memories with Wesley and feeling better without all of this swelling and pain. Fight for coming home to us and being a family."

That was when she searched my face. The words "home" and "family" struck a nerve. The two things she always wanted more than anything but could never find. I felt a tinge of anger in that moment. Toward God, toward the cancer cells invading her body, toward fate that dealt her and Wesley such tragedy. Trish was dying, and now she had the chance for what she had always dreamed of, but for how long? Surely, not long enough.

"I want to do so much with Wesley," she uttered, catching another tear with her finger. "I want us to have a home and a family. If this will give us time to share that together, then I want to do it. I do."

I reached out and hugged her, feeling both victory and sadness. We'd be family and get through this together. But I couldn't stop sensing the dark clouds moving in. We'd add more time and memories. We'd keep living our story, but for certain, there would be no happy ending.

Arlene and Margaret came into the room a few minutes later with warm greetings and genuine care in their eyes. I extended a chair for Arlene. Margaret perched on the end of Trish's bed. My stress level immediately eased. These women were the best of the best and would help Trish understand the new route we'd be taking.

As they talked and fielded Trish's questions, I realized it was a totally unfamiliar experience being on the other side of the chart listening in as a family member rather than as a medical profes-sional. I had a new perspective and sympathy for what a patient's loved ones went through when dealing with serious illness and a terminal diagnosis. It felt overwhelming, but I found it helpful to take all of this from my nursing perspective as well, where each and every discipline is so vital to a patient's journey. It never took just one person to make the difference, but instead a valuable team, all courageous and strong in their own right, fighting for the same common cause of keeping the patient as comfortable as possible. These discussions were part of the job before. I was used to the in-tensity and the emotion, but as I watched Trish soaking it all in and laying out a plan for the last phase of her life, it was as if a part of me were withering away with her. Now that it was personal, I learned that terminal illness also crept into a part of the family's soul where they died a little bit every day, too.

"This is not about giving up," I reminded her with conviction at the end of the conversation. "This is about living as well as you can for as long as you can to give you the gift of quality time."

Trish finally agreed. We had a new plan and were on the same page. I was so thankful for the compassion and expertise that Margaret and Arlene contributed to help Trish feel more at ease.

I began to see blending our two families wasn't something Dan or I could do alone. To get it done right, it was going to take a village.

Our next visit was with Kim, the care coordinator from Homeland Hospice. Her manner was kind, gentle, and very reassuring. She gave Trish and me information about all of their services, equipment, and such. With this new approach, we needed them in our corner.

Trish seemed pleased with the plan, and we were ready to start moving full speed ahead to get her home and acclimated to the new surroundings. This was uncharted territory—no one knew for sure if we had a week, a month, or, with a leap of faith, perhaps longer. I constantly prayed and pleaded with God that He would grant us time. Time for Trish and Wesley to be together. I thought the sweet country air would be cleansing and strengthening for both of them. Would having a new family to love and care for Trish just as she dreamed her entire life perhaps be the best medicine of all? I also asked God for guidance so we could grow closer to Wesley. We needed a chance to form some kind of trusting, caring relationship so that when his mommy left this earth, we would have a foundation to build on. Having time was key and what I kept praying for so passionately. But would this little boy ever accept us as his forever family?

Even though I experienced so many questions and a bit of cold feet, Dan and I knew, along with our children, that moving both

Trish and Wesley into our home was exactly what God was leading us to do. It was His will and our calling. It was why Trish and I were so powerfully drawn to each other. It was the plan He designed, tossing away the one we had made for ourselves. Was it scary? Oh, yes. Did I question if this would work? Many times. Was it a perfect happily ever after? Not by a longshot, but that's the thing about traveling along unfamiliar and unexpected terrain. Your steps feel unsteady, and there are many peaks and valleys, but the destination is what matters in the end.

CHAPTER 13

One Big Happy Family

May 17, 2014, was the big day Trish would officially join our household. Wesley had been staying with us since the night when she was first admitted to the hospital. My family tried their best to entertain and keep him happy until we could bring his mom home. We also discussed the new plan privately with our kids, but this time there was a little more hesitation mixed in with their willingness. Having Wesley here was one thing; he was like another sibling that blended well into the mix. But bringing in a dying mother who needed medical equipment and constant care, not knowing how long she had left to live . . . well, it scared them, especially Jenna.

"I've talked with her whenever they came over and I like Trish a lot," she confessed, swiping dark bangs from her brow. "But it's just hard to get close when I know she's going to die."

I rubbed circles on her back as I sat next to her on the living room sofa. "That's perfectly understandable," I said, remembering I was the only one in the room who dealt with the sick and dying on a regular basis. In truth, it was never something you ever got used to. "I just think it will take time to let that wall down and allow a friendship to develop."

"I don't want to see it happen," Noah said, as Emma and Anna nodded. "She's real nice, and I like my brother, but I'm kind of scared, too. I don't want to see her die."

Dan leaned forward in the chair next to us. "We aren't taking care of Trish until the end. Once her illness reaches a point where we can't keep her comfortable, she'll be admitted into a hospice facility."

"We want us all to be family and for Trish to enjoy being here for as long as she is able to be functional," I added. "But we won't be able to help her when her illness is in the end stages. I promise you guys, that is when she will be transported to a place that will be able to take care of her from there."

It grew quiet. I examined each of their expressions and tried to read their whirlwind of thoughts. My focus lingered the longest on Jenna, who seemed the most uneasy out of the group. She always had a fear of death as far back as I could remember. I didn't know why, exactly. She never really experienced a loss, but it was something she knew I dealt with in my work. I often went to the funerals of some of my closest patients. Even then, when she knew I was dressing in dark colors and getting ready to leave for the wake, she'd withdraw to her room as if the shadow of death would taint her somehow.

"I'm happy she's coming," Jenna finally said, giving in to a smile. "It will be fun to spoil her and pamper her and do her nails and stuff."

Noah scowled. "That's for girls. I'm going to show her how to catch lightning bugs in a jar, and me and Wesley are going to use them for a nightlight."

I chuckled and felt relief. The tension in the air just evaporated.

Anna got up and gave me a wonderful hug. "And we'll play piano for her. I bet she likes music. We'll maybe teach her how to play if she doesn't know how to already."

"She'll love that," I responded, soaking in the newfound excitement that was flowing.

Still, there was one thing that didn't come up but sat like an elephant in the room. The toughest part of this transition meant letting Wesley know the truth about his mother's condition. Otherwise, the kids would have to walk on eggshells, fearing they would somehow say the wrong thing or Wesley would accidentally find out the wrong way. He still had no idea and just knew she was very, very sick. Once she was settled in, Dan and I decided we'd get Pastor Mott and people from hospice involved to discuss with Trish how important it was to have complete honesty with Wesley during this time. On a few occasions during her last two hospital stays, Trish spoke about telling Wesley. She knew that it was the right thing to do for his sake and for her peace of mind, yet there was never the right time. Never the right words.

That's why we felt getting her here and becoming a blended family-

> *We'd be here until the tears all ran dry.*

ily would offer the support she needed. How Wesley would react once he knew the truth haunted my thoughts, but at least he now had loving arms to embrace him. We'd be here until the tears all ran dry.

I shared the situation about Wesley with the kids before we broke up our meeting. Thankfully, they were very understanding and knew not to make mention of Trish being terminal. They had come to adore Wesley and would never want to hurt him. For now, until he and his mother had that crucial conversation, we would all keep quiet.

On the day Trish was to come home, our team worked like a well-oiled machine. Robbin drove Trish to the apartment to pack up the things she would need, while I went to the store to get bedding and towels. I wanted everything to be perfect so I hunted for anything purple, Trish's favorite color. At home, Dan added a door to our TV room and covered the glass with Con-Tact paper to give Trish privacy. We put the hospital bed in place, and Jenna, Emma, and Anna helped to put on the new pretty floral purple sheets, matching fluffy pillows, and a cuddly lavender fleece blanket. Her bedside table had a purple glass vase filled with fragrant lilacs. Emma also placed on the table the honorary gold bell given to those in our household who are sick so they can give it a ring when they need anything. We also set up a basket with tissues, ChapStick, and the TV remote. Wesley added his own special touch by placing some of his most special stuffed animals on Mommy's new bed. The room was bright and filled with natural light from two large windows framed with ruffled curtains. The view looks out over the front of our house onto the porch. There Trish and I would soon sit in the white rockers, taking in the countryside, having laughs and heart-to-heart talks, and sipping tall glasses of iced tea. We moved the couch out of the room to make space for Trish's bed but kept the love seat so there was a nice place to sit for visitors or if Wesley just wanted to be near to his mother. The girls organized her bathroom, laying out fresh towels and arranging fragrant lavender soaps in a dish. Emma, Wesley, and Noah were in charge of decorations and put purple balloons on the white cabinets around her TV. The cherry on top was the giant "Welcome Home" sign made by the kids in colored marker and crayons that hung over Trish's bed, with every member of the family represented, including the two dogs. We certainly made up one big, happy clan! It was a ton of work and it felt as if we were preparing for royalty, but I wanted her to love it. It meant the world to me to give Trish a beautiful place to call her own and for her to know how much she was loved.

It was late evening when Robbin's car rolled up. Wesley especially was grinning and hopping up and down, waiting for the front door to open. It had been a long wait. In fact, a bit longer than we had anticipated due to the fact that Robbin and Trish had gotten lost between the highway and our house, since it was pitch dark without any streetlights. Robbin was frazzled because they had packed Trish's medication in the back of the car and didn't know just where it was buried. Robbin was afraid to stop since it was impossible to see and chances were they wouldn't be able to find the prescription bottle anyway, so she pushed ahead and finally made it to our driveway. But as we waited inside feeling excited and festive, ready to welcome our new family member home, Trish was a bit green around the gills from driving so long and not having her pills. As soon as she got out of the car, she leaned over and vomited on the driveway. It wasn't exactly the entrance she wanted to make, but all that mattered was that she was here. We brought her inside, sat her down, and got her a cold drink to help settle her stomach. Once she caught her breath and felt a bit better, we gathered and did as we had rehearsed, shouting in unison, "Welcome home!" She perked up and seemed ecstatic as we gave her the grand tour of her bedroom and bathroom. We all stood around her in a loving circle, Wesley glowing with his little arms wrapped around her waist.

"What do you think?" I asked. "Do you like it?"

The muscles in her chin quivered as tears ran down both cheeks. "I never had anything so nice," she answered. "It's all just absolutely perfect. Look at all the purple!" She then burst out crying and hugged each one of us. If I could have bottled that moment, I would have.

Robbin was getting ready to make the drive back but stopped so we could share an embrace. "We did it," I said, overcome with joy. "She's home. She's finally home."

Once everyone got settled in for the night, I went into Trish's room, where I tucked her in and made sure

> *"We did it," I said, overcome with joy. "She's home. She's finally home."*

Wesley was comfortable on the air mattress beside her. I leaned over and kissed Trish on the forehead.

"Good night, Dolly," I said, my spirit overflowing with all we'd accomplished. "I love you. You are home."

"Dolly?" She gave a little grin. "Is that my new nickname?"

I didn't know where it came from. It simply slipped out now that she was here and we were officially family. Yet looking at her, that's exactly what she seemed like to me. A beautiful little doll that you would treasure and admire and take care of.

"Yep. You'd better get used to it."

Trish laughed. "Still the bossy nurse."

Next, I kissed Wesley and said a prayer with him, a routine we'd begun the first night he was here.

Once all the kids had gone to bed, I lay next to my husband, snuggling against him in the darkness. It was hard to fall asleep—I was still wired and unable to relax after all the excitement. I was having pangs of fear, too.

"Can we do this?" I asked, my voice a bit fragile. "You know things will never be the same around here from this point forward."

He stroked my hair. "God gave us Trish and Wesley, and they are now our family. If things aren't the same, it means they weren't supposed to be. Sometimes change makes everyone's lives better."

> *"God gave us Trish and Wesley, and they are now our family. If things aren't the same, it means they weren't supposed to be."*

"Are you scared?" I asked. Dan was always logical and put together, not one to let his feathers get ruffled. But, then again, he'd never had a dying woman and her son move into his home before. A son that would be ours to raise one day, brokenhearted and all.

"Are you?" The old "answer a question with a question" technique.

I dug deep, searching my soul. I thought I'd say, "Yes . . . actually, Dan, I'm terrified!" But instead it was as if God's presence settled on the bed next to me—my strength, my light in the storm, my leader and protector. I knew He'd see us through this new journey. I also knew this dying mother and her son sleeping one floor below us belonged here in some unexplainable way. I felt it from the day Trish learned she was terminal and asked us to raise her little boy.

"No," I finally replied, feeling stronger than expected. "I can't fear what is obviously God's plan. I guess it's more a case of butterflies."

Dan gave an exhausted stretch and pulled me closer so I could lay my head on his chest. "Well, that works out perfectly since you've always loved butterflies."

I smiled. "And you," I whispered.

The move and excitement had drained Trish to the point that she was too weak to get out of bed the following day. It was a Sunday, so Dan took all the kids to the morning church service, and I stayed behind to keep an eye on her. Pastor Mott and his wife asked Dan if it would be all right if a group from church came by for a special visit that evening. They knew Trish and Wesley were now officially living with us and wanted to form a prayer circle around the outside of our home. It was their way of helping and making Trish feel uplifted. As the sun set, I could hardly wait and kept looking out the windows. Then I saw them. A string of cars lined our little street, and groups of people from our congregation gathered on our front lawn where Trish could see all the festivities from her bed. They all began to pray for our family and to bless our house. Pastor Mott and Joyce came inside and sat with Trish, sharing prayer and giving their personal welcome to our community. At the end of their visit, I went outside to join everyone on the front yard near Trish's bedroom window to sing hymns and praise songs, lifting hope and blessings into the wind. I sang along, this moment one of pure love. Trish was watching, just absorbing it all, her spirit renewed note by note.

As Trish got her strength back in the next couple of days, she turned into a completely different person. Instead of being groggy and sleepy, staying tucked underneath her lavender blanket, she began to eat a bit better, enjoyed watching TV, shared laughs, and seemed far more alert. She assembled a "To Do" list and was ready to tackle each item one by one. She wanted to turn off her electric at the apartment and figure out how to move out all their belongings by the end of the month when the lease was up. She also initiated contact with an attorney to get her will drawn up and completed. There were so many details to think about, and she was more than eager to check off each one now that she was feeling better.

On top of the priority list was getting Wesley enrolled into his new school, since he had missed an entire week already. Because I had no legal rights as his guardian at this point, Trish had to take him and handle the paperwork. So off we went as I pushed Trish in her wheelchair to meet personally with the principal. As it happened, on that particular morning it was a picnic day and the entire student body was at the park, leaving the school empty. This gave us the opportunity to tour the building so Trish could see everything and ask all kinds of questions. Once we were finished exploring, a petite woman with a warm smile came out of the lobby and introduced herself as Kate Zimmerman, Wesley's new teacher. I knew her well already because both Emma and Noah had her as their teacher in second grade. She'd be perfect to help break the ice for Wesley, who was growing shyer by the second. Mrs. Zimmerman winked at Trish and then stooped down to Wesley's level.

"I'm looking forward to having you in my class." Her tone was light and inviting. She had already been briefed on what was going on with Trish's health and the fact that they were moving into our home. "The students just came back from a trout release at the park and will be heading into their classrooms. I'd love it if you stayed and finished out the rest of the day with us. Would you like that?"

Wesley didn't expect anything more than a brief look at his new school. He definitely didn't want to leave his mother and be alone in a strange place. He pulled back, gripped on to the wheelchair, and formed his lips in a pout. It looked like he had no plans to budge.

"It will be fine," Trish assured him, tugging his arm toward the teacher. "They're very nice here. You'll do okay, Wesley. It's just for a few hours."

"Can't I come home with you?" he whispered against her ear, well aware he had to act like a big boy in front of Mrs. Zimmerman.

"You have to go to school, Wesley. You've missed too much already," Trish answered, slicking down a piece of his hair and trying to ignore the quivering muscles in his chin.

It was a tough moment. I didn't know what my boundaries were. I was supposed to be Wesley's mother one day, yet for now,

I was to stay on the outskirts. If I took over and tried to comfort him, I'd be stealing Trish's job away, yet if I didn't do anything and stood still as a statue, Wesley may not ever come to learn that I cared.

Finally, when he lingered too long and Trish seemed flustered, I knelt down and met his gaze. "You know, Noah and Emma both go here, too. They'll be so surprised to see you and ride the bus home with you today. That will be really fun, won't it?"

His frown eased up a bit, and then he nodded. Trish sighed with relief. The two of us made a good team.

"Okay, now. Go on, go on." Trish hugged him, but he kept reaching out to hug her once again. "You're fine. You're going to make great new friends, and you'll come home and tell me all about it."

Mrs. Zimmerman extended her hand, and finally Wesley took hold. He twisted his neck back to look at his mother. He was on the verge of tears, and I knew if Trish caught sight of just one teeny, tiny droplet, she'd crumble. This was one of those critical moments, like ripping off a Band-Aid. It had to be done quickly or it would be much more painful. I grabbed hold of the handles on the wheelchair, waved to Wesley, and swiveled Trish toward the exit doors, pushing her about as fast as I could without breaking into a run. Once we got outside in the fresh air, I felt I could finally breathe again. I hadn't realized how stressful it was for the two of them to part ways. If it was that hard just for an afternoon, what will this poor child do once their good-bye was forever?

"He'll be fine," Trish said, consoling herself out loud as I wheeled her toward the van. "He's going to have a great day."

"He will," I agreed, still heavy in the corners of my soul where I secretly wondered how many great days were left for Wesley, Trish, and our new family.

LEFT: Trish, Wesley, and Molly the dog at Robbin's house (June 2014).

ABOVE: Wesley and Molly the dog (June 2014).

ABOVE: The boys: Parker, Wesley, Owen, and Noah.

LEFT: Noah and Wesley—best friends.

ABOVE: Two mothers, one well-loved little boy!

LEFT: Trish and me.

ABOVE: Our family on a trip to show Trish the beach one last time at Fenwick Island, Delaware.

LEFT: Kayaking together at Fenwick Island, Delaware, in 2014.

LEFT: Oldest to youngest, right to left: Anna, Jenna, Emma, Noah, Owen, Wesley, Parker, and Addy at the beach.

RIGHT: Trish in her beach wheelchair with my brother, Adam. "Does he come with the chair?"

LEFT: Me holding Minnie, Emma's kitten.

RIGHT: The Maryland girls! Left to right: Teresa, Sue, Trish, Maria, and Laureen visiting Trish at our house.

ABOVE: Robbin, Trish, and I getting ready to go to NYC for a day to make Trish feel special.

LEFT: Robbin, Trish, and me at the famous Kleinfeld Bridal in NYC.

RIGHT: Trish's dream come true—meeting Randy from TLC's *Say Yes to the Dress!*

LEFT: Trish in the Big Apple.

RIGHT: Wesley and Noah at Lego's Brick Fest.

LEFT: Trish and Milo the cat.

RIGHT: Wesley, the little fisherman!

ABOVE: One of the miniature carousel horses Trish loved to collect.

RIGHT: The cross necklace Trish gave to me for my birthday— this gift touched my heart so much!

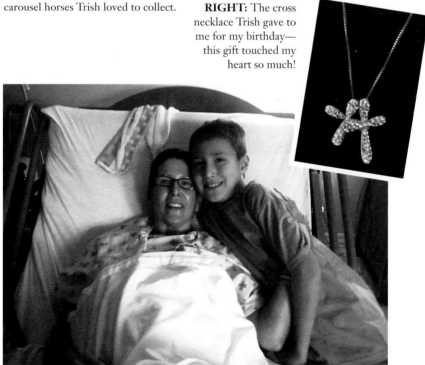

ABOVE: Trish and Wesley in the hospital room.

ABOVE: Celebrating Trish's last Mother's Day in 2014 (©Tadpole Photography).

ABOVE: An unbreakable bond between mother and son (©Tadpole Photography).

CHAPTER 14

A Circle of Kindness

It has always fascinated me how a rainbow forms. In order to see this breathtaking sight, you need two ingredients: sunlight and raindrops. There must first be dark clouds followed by a downpour, and then when the sun peeks through, those warm golden rays penetrate the raindrops and create an awesome arc of colors that stretches across the sky. In other words, something beautiful appears because of a storm. And that's exactly what happened right here in our little town of McAlisterville.

In the coming days, we began to get donations of food from our loving church family. Laura, who is in charge of organizing meals for different functions, had an entire refrigerator reserved in the church kitchen with our name on it. She planned meals for my family on cards asking for meatloaf, macaroni and cheese, vegetables, and desserts. People would take an index card with a dish on it and by the following Sunday everything for the next week was made and packaged with cooking or reheating instructions written on the container. It was a huge blessing to load up our van after the service to keep our fridge stocked full for our growing clan. Trish had never seen so much food in her life and was overwhelmed by everyone's generosity. She also had never experienced Pennsylvania Dutch cooking and now had a newfound love! Before long, she was actually gaining some weight, and every pound looked wonderful on her.

It seemed the donation of meals was just the beginning. Our friends Dick and Janet stopped by the house bringing a mountain of paper products: everything from paper plates, cups, and plastic-ware. No washing dishes here! Then our mailbox began to fill each day with tons of notes and cards, all with loving wishes from friends, family, and church members, along with prayers for Wesley and Trish. Even flowers were delivered, which Trish loved to set in her room. This kind of instant love and attention was something she never imagined, and already it lifted her spirits. Everyone wanted to make sure she and Wesley felt welcomed into our family and that they knew they were loved and cared about.

The early weeks were a bit challenging. There were times when Dan had to be out of the house doing things for his job and I had to work at the hospital. The kids were in school, and we didn't want Trish to be alone, so several people from church, friends, and neighbors set time aside to come and stay with her. She was still very weak and needed assistance, so they would chat with her, prepare her lunch, fold the laundry, watch TV with her, and even keep track of her meds. Our entire family was experiencing acts of kindness from those around us. The cheerleading booster club at Anna's school put together a special basket made just for Wesley and delivered it personally. They filled it with all of his favorite snacks along with gift cards to restaurants in the area, mini-golf, and fun family activities. His face lit up at the generosity of the gift. I am forever humbled, thankful, and touched by the love we received from so many during that initial transition.

The more people heard about Trish and Wesley joining our family, the more these types of blessings came rolling in. The teachers from the school rallied together and took up a collection to show their support and well wishes. Wesley's teacher, Mrs. Zimmerman, and Emma's teacher, Mrs. Harris, came to the house one night and delivered a card along with a check that we would later use for some fun family outings. I just remember Trish blinking in total disbelief, hugging them, and saying, "Thank you, thank you, thank you!"

Another moment I look back on and will never forget was when Laura, my friend Mia, and many other family friends and members of the community got together to come up with an amazing surprise for Wesley. They knew from our scattered conversations that Wesley hadn't had much growing up and that he wanted an Xbox gaming system more than anything in the world. It tugged at their hearts that Trish had worked so hard, yet because of her illness, she wasn't able to afford expensive gifts. So the team rallied together, and Laura delivered the Xbox to Trish one day all wrapped with a bow on top of the package. They also bought an assortment of games to go with it, but there was one important catch in their scheme. The group didn't want Wesley to think it was from them. They wanted Trish to give it to him . . . from her. He was ecstatic as Trish savored his grateful hugs. Tears filled her eyes for reasons he would never know.

This is the thing. Life is very uncertain. Maybe being an oncology nurse makes me more aware of that. I see it every day. People who once were living life without a care—planning trips, aiming for that promotion at work, looking forward to having children or maybe grandchildren—get hit with the unexpected, and those plans disappear. Tragedy comes in many forms. Bad things happen out of the blue, to our bodies, to our finances, to our friends, family, and loved ones. To people on the other side of the world we read about in the newspaper headlines. But I witnessed something absolutely amazing in this journey with Trish and Wesley. Even when life throws you what appears to be its worst, there are blessings and love, hope and support, and proof that nothing can defeat the kindness of the human spirit. Difficult times bring out the good in people, and that's what counts most of all.

> *Even when life throws you what appears to be its worst, there are blessings and love, hope and support, and proof that nothing can defeat the kindness of the human spirit.*

I'll never forget that in those first few weeks as we were showered in such generosity, Trish kept telling me how lucky I was to have so many giving and caring friends. Up until then I felt so helpless, unable to cure her, give her time, or make a way so she could watch Wesley grow up. But in that moment I suddenly felt as if I could give her a gift that would stay with her forever.

"You know what, Trish," I told her, my joyful soul soaring to the moon. "These special friends are now your dear friends, too. You and Wesley are loved and no longer alone."

CHAPTER 15

No Place Like Walmart

The swelling in Trish's legs began going down due to the rest she'd been getting and the special hospital bed she'd been sleeping on. It had an air mattress that would redistribute her body weight and allow her to put her feet up. She was even able to walk short distances with a cane, which gave her a bit more independence. We still used the wheelchair for longer distances, but to her, even walking from her bedroom to her bathroom on her own was like an Olympic victory.

Trish did have her own special brand of humor, which never failed to amuse me, even when she felt worn out and was confined to her bed. She'd often get bored, so when I wasn't working at the hospital, I'd be entertainment for her. We'd talk, watch a DVD, and just hang out together. When I had to leave for work, it was a major letdown to her day. I was the one who doted on her the most, so if I wasn't there, my family checked in on her from time to time, but she was often alone, looking out her windows for the boys playing together in the front yard.

One day I got home from work and heard her call out from her room before I ever had the chance to put my purse down. "Oh, Tricia," she said, a melodramatic tone in her voice, "I don't like it when you work. Everybody forgets me when you're not here. I didn't even take my medicine until one o'clock today. I swear, if I died, the only way anyone would know something was wrong is if the flies started circling and swarming around my room."

I felt absolutely horrible but stifled a chuckle at the same time. Her graphic description of the whole thing was . . . well, very Trish. So I went to Dan and talked to him about it. He had been busy all day in the garage, where he and some other friends were renovating a section for his new home office.

"I did check in on her several times," he said in his defense. "She was out like a light. I thought if she could sleep through the buzzing of all those power tools right outside the window, who was I to wake her up?"

"But she's on timed medication. You can't just let her sleep. She needs her pain pills on a certain schedule."

He looked remorseful and shifted his stance. "I will from now on. I'm sorry. I didn't know."

We joked that he needed a manual called, "How to Juggle Taking Care of a Terminally Ill Woman While Using Power Tools"!

It was clear that Trish craved a lot of attention, which took some getting used to for all of us. We had life to attend to, but Trish only had time on her hands.

"It's on, Tricia," she'd yell to me. "*Say Yes to the Dress* is on! Have you ever seen it? It's where brides shop at this really fancy place in New York City called Kleinfeld Bridal. I never ever miss an episode. If we go out, I'll have to record it on the DVR. Look at this wedding gown! You've got to see it. I just love all that bling!"

I kept stirring the gravy, not wanting to scorch the bottom. "That sounds really pretty, Trish."

"Oh, look at this one. The lace is spectacular. I think it's too low-cut for her, though. Have you seen this show, Tricia?"

"I don't watch a lot of TV."

"Come watch with me!"

I laughed and finally took the pot off the burner. If there was one thing this woman was already teaching me, it was to steal little moments here and there. I wasn't one to do much of that—always being on the go.

So I walked in from the kitchen and plopped on the love seat across from her bed to see what all the fuss was about. She pointed wide-eyed at a young lady in a huge ivory ball gown stepping up on a pedestal to admire her reflection as the sales associates fastened a veil to her hair. It must have been the mother who was sitting and crying. I wondered if it was because her baby girl was getting married or the price tag that must come with such a dress.

"She looks like Cinderella," Trish cooed. "Look, see that guy in the expensive suit and glasses? That's Randy. He is such a sharp dresser and a real hoot. He's really so much fun. We'd hit it off so well, he and I. I just love him to pieces."

I found myself drawn more to Trish's expression than to the television screen. Her eyes were so sparkly and dancing with joy, transfixed on the bride-to-be while her hands sort of wrung together with exhilaration as she could hardly sit still. She might as well have been right there in that fancy bridal showroom, she was so caught up in this young girl's shopping experience. I never saw her like this before. She was like a child watching Cinderella all aglow with happily ever after's. It dawned on me as I studied her smile that had I continued with my kitchen duties as I usually did, this memory

> *This moment would be one I'd tuck away for safekeeping. These precious slivers of time would soon be gone. It was imperative that I absorbed every word, every mannerism, everything about her, while I still could.*

would have slipped right by me. I made a mental note not to take things quite so seriously and to make time to notice the little things. This moment would be one I'd tuck away for safekeeping. These precious slivers of time would soon be gone. It was imperative that I absorbed every word, every mannerism, everything about her, while I still could.

"Isn't it beautiful?" Trish asked, finally taking her focus from

New York City to the place where I sat. "Isn't this just the most magnificent thing you ever saw?"

"It is," I answered, knowing we were speaking about two different things. "I'm so glad you called me in here to see it. I wouldn't have wanted to miss it for anything in the world." And that was the absolute truth.

Once she felt better, all she wanted to do was go, go, go! The transformation was nothing short of miraculous. One of the first places I took her was to Anna and Jenna's chorus concert at school. She enjoyed the music and seeing the kids up onstage. Wesley stayed behind with Noah, more comfortable now with short spans away from his mother. He trusted she'd be coming back and there was no need to worry. With so many hospital stays where she left his sight and was gone for days on end, it was so good to watch him finally feel secure that things would be getting better now.

The following weekend Trish was still gaining speed and raring to go. She was blossoming now that she had a loving home, rest, good food, and the proper care. A new gleam seemed to shine in her eyes. She loved to go to events and went along with me to Anna's piano recital. No sooner was the last note played than she asked what else was on the agenda. She eagerly anticipated our next outing. This critically ill woman had somehow turned into a constant ball of motion! It was a blessing to see this transformation, but it soon evolved into a rather unexpected and worrisome tug of war.

"Hey, let's go out," Trish said one day as I went about my household chores. "It's gorgeous outside. Let's take off and do something."

I paused with my scrub pad, scouring the kitchen sink, and blew a strand of hair from my eyes. "Trish, I did a twelve-hour shift yesterday, so today I need to catch up on cleaning. I have a lot to get done this afternoon."

"It can wait."

"No, it can't."

She gave me that mischievous grin. "Put down the sponge. That's an order. Let's get out for a while."

And then it all came back to me. I was having this conversation with a woman who was dying of cancer and had no idea how many days she had left. Her priority list was different from mine. Suddenly, a sparkling clean sink didn't seem quite as important. To Trish's delight, I threw down the sponge, and we ended up browsing her favorite place—Walmart.

In reality, I didn't always give in, though. If I did, my home would have turned into a neglected disaster. After all, with a household of eight, if you didn't do laundry for a couple of days or the dishes sat after each meal, mole hills quickly turned into mountains. Besides that, I admit to liking things tidy or I get a bit on edge. But one afternoon while I dug in my heels and refused to give in to Trish's itch to get out into the world once again, she devised a plan that even I wasn't prepared for.

"Hey, Tricia . . . don't you think I could maybe just drive around here? Just take Wesley for a little spin? My car just sits out there abandoned. Don't you think it would be a fun idea?"

I stopped stuffing handfuls of wet clothes into the dryer and gaped at this woman before me. A woman on enough pain meds to put an elephant on its side was asking me what I thought of her getting behind the wheel of a four-thousand-pound vehicle.

"Seriously?"

She nodded. "Just a short drive. Right around here."

I straightened. God help me, but she was absolutely determined. "No doctor on Earth would authorize you to operate a vehicle on the amount of pain medication that you're taking. You're not a child and can do whatever you want to do, but I don't think it's a good idea. That's all I'll say."

She batted her lashes and twitched the muscle in her left cheek. "Well, then . . . I suppose."

Was that a yes or a no? Was she supposing she was an adult and could do as she pleased or was she seeing that I was the rational one here who was 100 percent in the right? Trying to shake off the conversation, I went back to loading the dryer, but out of my peripheral vision, I saw her go back to her room and turn the TV on. The keys were staying in her purse.

It soon became apparent that with Trish's newfound urge to be a busy bee, I had to come up with some reinforcements to keep her active. My sister-in-law, Jessica, was my heaven-sent angel who happily came over and took her places, mostly to her ultimate destination, Walmart. She'd get in a wheelchair so she could ride up and down the aisles, shopping and shopping, and then shopping some more. Trish was never as happy as when she was set loose among anything with a Walmart price tag. With her monthly disability check and no more rent and utilities to pay, she liked to splurge—buying new clothes for Wesley and herself, costume jewelry, nail polish, and knickknacks for her already too cluttered little bedroom.

If it wasn't Jessica or myself, then the designated driver would be Anna, who loved taking Trish and the kids to our local ice cream takeout store called the Creme Stop. Anybody who is anybody in McAlisterville always goes there for frozen treats. It's a small little shop where you step up to the window and order, then either sit and enjoy at the nearby picnic tables or eat your ice cream in the car. Trish loved having her appetite back and soon discovered her favorite was a large chocolate peanut butter milkshake. It even got to the point where she craved one every single day—she became a regular pretty quickly! All the teenage girls who worked there also knew Jenna and Anna, so they would know whenever we stopped by to have Trish's milkshake ready for her with a big grin. If one of us made the run without Trish, they always asked how she was. It was nothing short of service for a queen.

One day I took Trish to the Creme Stop to get her daily

must-have. We went up to the window, placed our order, and got our shakes. When we got back to the car, we both stopped and stared. Crisp ten-dollar bills lay right out in plain sight on the front seat.

"Trish, did you drop some money out of your wallet?" I asked.

She shook her head. "No. Are you sure Dan didn't leave that there?"

"He doesn't carry cash. Neither one of us do."

We kind of shrugged it off, a bit perplexed as we indulged in our ice cream and went on our way. But the cash fairy continued to visit on subsequent trips. One day my mother took Trish for her milkshake. As the two of them went up to the window to place their order, Trish glanced around and let her in on the little secret.

"You know, Teresa, you have to leave your window down here."

My mom raised her brows with surprise. "What? Why?"

"There will be money in your car when you get back."

Later my mother admitted she wasn't sure if it was the pain meds talking or what, so she simply nodded as if money appearing in cars was as normal as the summer rain.

Finally, there was the one day I took Trish for her shake. There was hardly anyone there. The first thing I thought when I saw the vacant parking lot was that we could quite possibly catch the secret messenger! When it was bustling with people from our neighborhood and church, it was always an impossible guess. It could have been anybody. Yet on this particular visit with barely a customer in sight, at least nobody that I recognized, we went through our usual motions of going up to the window and placing our ice cream orders. When we returned to the car, it was no surprise. Cash sat on the front seat.

Trish pointed and slurped her milkshake. "Yep, there it is."

I glanced around and still saw nobody there. "I'll be right back," I told her as I headed toward the window and tapped lightly on the glass. Matt, the owner, had been a longtime friend of mine since high school.

"Anything wrong with your order?" he asked nonchalantly.

"Matt, there's an interesting phenomenon happening every time that I've been visiting your place of business. We come to the window, we order our ice cream, and then go back to the car and there's money on the seat. Would you happen to know anything about that?"

His eyes just filled up with tears as he looked over my shoulder to where Trish was now sitting, no doubt halfway finished with her gigantic milkshake. "I just wanted to do something to help," he said with a sheepish grin.

Now it was my turn to spring a leak as I quickly swiped the wetness from my cheeks. If I could have jumped through that little window and given him a huge hug, I would have. "That is one of the most kind, generous things," I choked out. "She just loves eating here. I don't even know how to thank you."

Wracked with emotion, he waved me on my way. I knew he was

too proud for me to make a fuss. When I returned to the car, Trish crinkled her forehead and asked if everything was okay.

"Everything is perfect," I honestly replied. More perfect than I ever imagined.

After Trish passed away, one of the first times I took Wesley to the Creme Stop this past spring, he went right up to the counter and ordered his mommy's large chocolate peanut butter milkshake. He knew exactly what he wanted. It brought a lump to my throat. She may have been gone, but never forgotten.

After her first couple of weeks with us, Trish got exciting news. Her brother, Ollie, and his wife, Erin, along with her girlfriends from Baltimore were going to make a road trip to meet us and see her new home. I made a huge spread so we could have a wonderful picnic lunch and looked forward to meeting everyone. Before the gang arrived, Trish gave me a few background details. Teresa, Laureen, and Sue were dear friends. Maria was Trish's rock during her parents' deaths—she was a bit older than Trish, yet they'd been beloved friends for nearly twenty years. The bond and cherished memories Trish held deep down inside put an unmistakable glow to her face as she spoke.

"I'm surprised you wouldn't consider Maria to be the one to take care of Wesley," I said, now knowing how very close the two women were.

Trish shook her head. "Well, she's never been married or had children of her own. Although I know she'd do anything and would be happy to help, Maria works and it's not her lifestyle to be a mom. She does love him dearly, but it just wouldn't make for a good fit."

"Well," I said, patting her knee. "I think God already has it all worked out."

The visit was glorious. I adored Ollie and Erin, who were eager to help us in any way they could to get Trish settled and taken care of. The ladies shared stories of the good old days, which made Trish laugh until she cried. Maria was striking with her red hair and a dark suntan—she was delightful and confident, and knew how to take command of a room. At the end of the day, after all of the food was put away and the conversations began to wind down, we planned to get together again the following Saturday to pack up Trish's apartment. I dreaded that day because I knew how emotionally difficult it would be for Trish and Wesley. It was the first real step for them to say good-bye to life together as they knew it.

CHAPTER 16

Nesting

Imagine there's a powerful hurricane coming your way and you have to evacuate suddenly. You must leave the place that was your life—your home—filled with memories and belongings. You have little time. You can bring with you only a few sentimental items and some basic needs. The rest will be gone forever. Welcome to Trish and Wesley's moving day.

I unwisely agreed to let Wesley come along. He should have stayed behind with my brother and sister-in-law like the rest of the kids, but he wanted to pack his own things. I just didn't know how attached he'd be to every single item. Trish had this same mentality, and it was difficult to get them to let go of their possessions. Thankfully, Robbin joined us once she got out of work, along with Trish's friends from Maryland, her neighbor, and another lady from her most recent job. Dan and Ollie were there to handle the heavy items. We had quite a crew to get the job done and a U-Haul to bring back anything Trish wanted to keep.

Starting in the kitchen, Erin and I got rid of just about everything. There were a few choice items we wrapped carefully for Trish to keep, such as nice dishes and a few fragile wineglasses that belonged to her mom. The fine line we were going to have to walk during this expedition was separating the sentimental must-haves and needs from the items that would get donated. That line got easily blurred.

The longer the hours dragged on, the more I realized what a job this would be. Every nook and cranny of this apartment was filled. Trish and Wesley had enough clothing for four people. I'd watch Trish bag up clothes, then think twice and take things out. Each and every decision to donate or to keep was absolutely grueling. Finally, Sue took Wesley to McDonald's to help entertain him for a while, since we didn't seem to be making progress. If he stayed in charge of packing up every one of his things, we would get nowhere. Once the coast was clear, Maria went to Wesley's room along with Dan and me. We tried to keep special toys from his babyhood, but most of those we found were missing parts, broken, or from a fast-food restaurant.

"Is this important?" Maria held up a little plastic robot, staring at it as if it were a science experiment gone wrong. "I don't know. I never had kids. There's just too much here! Way, way too much!"

I tried to help her before she had a complete meltdown, cramming all that we could into donation bags.

Trish began to get very agitated and started gathering a bunch of home décor and lamps, as much as her arms could hold. I told her she didn't need them. There was simply no room. It was about the thousandth time I said those exact words that day. This time it pushed her over the brink as she started to grind her molars.

"You wait," she snapped, hugging her items even closer. "I'm going to prove you guys all wrong. I'm going to live and then I'm going to have nothing left. Just nothing!"

I wanted to crumble. I didn't know what was harder—seeing her try so desperately to hold on to the things that meant home or to hear her in denial over her being terminally ill. I'd never heard her question her diagnosis before. Was it normal for her to think this was all a mistake? Then again, there could be nothing normal when you're dying and grasping so frantically to stay. This day was proof she and Wesley were facing the end. It had to be too much reality for her. For that instant, I tried to put myself in her shoes. Strangers rummaging through my house going through everything I owned. Telling me what was being donated and what I could keep, all while reminding me there wasn't much room. When, really, what it must have reminded her was that there wasn't much time left.

"I'm sorry, Dolly," I said, using the nickname that had made her smile before. "I know how difficult this must be for you. I just don't know how to make it any easier."

She glanced at the things bundled in her arms and then slowly set them down. "Unfortunately, that's something we have in common because neither do I."

As high as everyone's frustration levels got as we finally finished the job, I felt deeply sorry for Trish and Wesley. This was once their home, now cluttered and a complete mess, but home just the same. These things that were getting donated, thrown out, or going in storage were like pieces of their life being taken away. Every lamp, every bit of clothing, every stuffed animal was once something that at least belonged to them. At the end of the day, as Trish got in our van, exhausted with her legs swollen and hurting, I just felt dark inside. Once the door was closed and we were on the road to McAlisterville, their life in that apartment was officially history.

"You okay?" I glanced at Trish as we drove away.

"It was a glorious day," she exclaimed, to my surprise. "I loved seeing everybody and, to tell you the honest truth, I actually got out of there with a lot more than I thought I was going to!"

I burst out laughing, feeling my love for her grow. She was tough and spirited. She could look heartache straight in the face and somehow come out on top with more spunk than anyone I'd ever known. Now, the hundreds of VHS tapes, CDs, and random memorabilia were on their way to my home to go only God knew where. But, in reality, it was no longer just my home—it was Trish's and Wesley's, too. Somehow, we'd make it all work.

> *But, in reality, it was no longer just my home—it was Trish's and Wesley's, too. Somehow, we'd make it all work.*

At that point, Trish began nesting. I think it was important for her to add her touch to our house to feel included. She continuously moved back and forth from the garage, where we stored the things we'd moved for her, and brought more and more inside. By the time I returned home one night from a long shift at the hospital, I didn't recognize the interior of my own house. It jolted me at first. I had my surroundings just so, but I knew how important it was to allow Trish to feel genuinely a part of this family. The first thing I noticed was how she personalized the refrigerator. I usually kept it clean and orderly, with only a few family photos and a calendar. Now every square inch was covered with photographs, Wesley's drawings, and magnets that meant something to her. She also placed the accessories from her kitchen in Maryland—which had a fifties theme—across the counters and on the island. They were all chrome and strawberries, her mom's very favorite.

Then there was the toilet paper tree in my bathroom, which could only mean she ran out of room in hers. In the living room, a multitude of sun catchers hung in all of the windows. I didn't say anything at first. It was so much to take in, but one thing was very clear. I was losing control. This wasn't my style or how I liked to keep things.

I went to speak with Trish about my frustration, but once I got to her room I froze. She had taken pushpins and decorated the walls with hundreds of assorted pictures. As I tried to walk a few feet forward, I quickly realized that the things she dragged in from the garage now made it even impossible to step inside. The mountain of DVDs and CDs along with her decorative items nearly made me hyperventilate until I reminded myself to stop and count my blessings. At least there was no sign of the Elvis memorabilia I knew filled one of her boxes. I later learned she had also taken over both of the downstairs coat closets: one for her summer wardrobe and the other for the fall. As I stood at the door of Trish's room, I mentally counted to ten to force myself to calm down. I had to see it from her side. This was her way of still having a sense of control. I dragged my gaze from even more shoes in her closet to Trish's glowing expression.

"I don't think we can reasonably fit anything more into this house, Trish. Maybe you'll have to slow down a bit. What's out in the garage should stay in the garage."

She nodded, still looking contented. "Well, this is all I need. I think this is good."

All I could do was press a smile on my lips as I pivoted and left the room. "I think I can, I think I can, I think I can," I muttered under my breath.

CHAPTER 17

Time Out

We could no longer avoid telling Wesley the truth about his mother's illness. Trish agreed it was time. We called on our church counselor, Pastor Joe, to counsel Trish on how to go about it and give her support and prayer. I remember the day she went into Wesley's room and closed the door behind them. She told me she held him in her arms and delicately explained how Mommy's cancer wasn't getting any better despite the medication she had taken to try to fight it. She told him that Dan and I, along with the kids, were the family God had chosen to love him and raise him once she went to heaven. He cried, holding on to her. Words made it real. Trish then asked him if he was happy with us here, if he felt comfortable living in this house, and if he wanted to stay. According to Trish, he answered, "I love it here. I want to stay another twenty years!" That was all she needed to have the peace she was looking for. I think she knew that in a way it would make it easier to let go one day. Once it was over and they emerged, Wesley had dried his tears and went off to play with Noah. Trish seemed relieved and even said it was as if he knew all along. I remembered when he got so sick in the bushes at the gas station the first time we spent the day together and he met the family. I believe he knew, too. His keen instincts told him his mother was dying and big changes were coming. Wesley didn't seem to dwell on their talk. He didn't seem depressed or lock himself in his room. Instead, he went back to being Wesley. The more I observed him, the more I saw what a strong, courageous, and accepting little boy he was. The seed of love for him had already been planted in the depths of my heart. All it needed was time and patience for it to sprout and grow.

There were a lot of days when I would be working and unable to take Trish places she needed or wanted to go. This was when I called in my task force, whom I still consider miracle workers. We had wonderful helpers from hospice who took Trish to her doctor's appointments. These precious elderly volunteers would drive an hour each way and do it happily, just to lend a hand. Jessica continued to be on call, as did Tanya, who went to our church. They were both my angels, always willing to pitch in to lighten the load. Tanya formed an especially close bond with Trish, since she is a breast cancer survivor. They would chat away like girlfriends as she drove Trish and Wesley to appointments, McDonald's, and shopping. Ultimately, that friendship would forever impact Tanya's life. Inspired by knowing Trish, this past year she got a job on our unit and now works at Pinnacle as a nursing assistant. We often think back on the incredible impact this one woman had on so many people.

One day in June, Trish went from being happy and this bundle of energy to being very angry. She stopped talking to me and didn't hang around the kids much. I even noticed the snacks in the pantry that she bought for herself and for Wesley had their names written on them with a Sharpie marker. I never questioned. I knew she was trying to separate what was theirs, but it hurt. I didn't like the division. In the Seaman household, everyone shared everything. That's what families do.

"What's going on, Trish?" I eventually asked her, not understanding the snippy attitude. "Did I do something to offend you?"

She tapped her nails on the counter, looking off in the distance with a scowl on her lips. "I'm tired of everyone taking everything away from me. I have no independence anymore. I need people too much. I hate having everyone treating me like I'm helpless. This is no way to live."

Maybe it was because I was tired to the bone after a long shift, or maybe it was because we were standing in a beautiful home where she had the best of everything at her disposal. The people who were taking her places were people who truly loved and cared about her. Her attitude rubbed me the wrong way.

"You've got a great support team, Trish. They are here to make things easier on you, not make you feel helpless."

"I feel trapped. We have nothing of our own anymore. Our lives go according to your schedules now. Is this how I'm going to spend the rest of my time? If so, it will be totally miserable."

Now I was upset. I wanted to yell out, "I can't live like this, either!" as loud as I could, but instead I clamped my jaw tight and left the room. I went for a drive in my car away from the house to cool down. I dialed Maria's number and impatiently counted the rings before she picked up.

"So she's feeling like a prisoner or something. I don't know, Maria. I've done everything I can possibly do, yet she's angry and acting like she can't handle it here anymore. She's been so upset and short with everyone."

"It's nothing you've done wrong, Tricia. She just found out she's dying. You have to expect her to go through a lot of phases."

"I don't know how to juggle it or keep everyone happy while helping my children adjust to having two new people in their home. A home we hardly recognize anymore."

She groaned. "Oh, wow. I can just picture it if it's anything like that apartment, but it's going to get better. You're all still getting used to each other."

"That's one of the things we disagreed about the other night. I told her we need to compromise on some things, like how Wesley is allowed to do whatever it is he wants while the other children have to follow rules and bedtimes."

"Trish has to understand that. You all have to be on the same page."

"We're chapters apart," I said in exasperation.

"That's rough," she said. "How late does Wesley stay up?"

"He'll be up all night long," I answered, my voice escalating as I kept driving the backcountry roads to nowhere. "He plays games at night while she watches TV or shops online at Walmart, which is another thing that needs to get under control. She sleeps during the day, but he's exhausted all the time."

"You do need to set boundaries. That's not good for anyone, especially Wesley."

"Exactly, but telling Trish that is a different story. If we are somehow going to integrate him into our lives, he has to somewhat follow the same rules that the other kids follow. If not, this whole thing doesn't have a chance of working. I'm at my wits' end."

There was a moment of silence. I could just about hear Maria's wheels turning. If anyone could come up with a solution, I knew it was the one who knew Trish the longest.

"I think we need to bring her down here for a bit," she said. "Just to get her out and away for a couple of days. I can even take some time off from work. Maybe Teresa, Laureen, and I can all do things with her down in Baltimore. We'll get her out for a fun little trip."

"Do you think it will help?"

"I think you both need some space since it's been a pretty intense month. Let me work my magic and when I send her back home, she'll be as sweet as spun sugar."

Maria was a godsend—the perfect person to calm me down in my frustration. We went on to plan the trip for the following week. The girls would pick up Trish for her doctor's appointment in Harrisburg, then go on to Baltimore from there for four days. Wesley would stay with us, which would be the true test. Without Trish there, I could exercise my right as a parent to get him to abide by household rules and do things the Seaman way. To my amazement, once Trish was off on her girlfriends' trip, Wesley did perfectly fine. He listened. He was obedient. He learned to sleep in his bunk bed. I made the decision to take the air mattress away from Trish's room to encourage him to sleep in Noah's room. It wasn't a complete success because as soon as his mother returned, he moved back into bed with her, which I understood. Every moment was still so precious for them, but I didn't move the air mattress back. Enabling wasn't going to get us anywhere if we were going to move this little boy toward any kind of normalcy.

As it turned out, it was a nice and well-needed break. Trish had a ball with her friends, and our family enjoyed falling into place and seeing how effortlessly Wesley followed our rules, almost as if he had been hungering for a schedule.

Once Trish returned, I was a bit of a mess, not knowing what to expect. I still felt uncomfortable from the words we'd said to each other, and on her first night back, it was pretty awkward. Neither of us knew quite what to say or how to act.

Finally, Trish faced me with an apologetic look on her face. "I never meant to argue with you."

My walls tumbled down. I couldn't stay angry with this woman who was dealing with so much.

"I just think we both needed some time," I admitted. "You've had to move your whole life and give up so much while we needed to regroup after having new people coming into our home. It's definitely a fine balance trying to figure out how to allow you to keep your independence as much as possible and to maintain the order and the flow to the way things are done in our family so you don't feel like you're losing. I want you to feel like you're gaining, Trish. I want you to be happy and enjoy it here."

Thankfully, the rising temper and her need to lash out before going to Baltimore were nowhere to be seen. Now, her eyes were soft, her posture relaxed, and she was no longer in attack mode. I began to grow hopeful.

"This is a lot of change for everyone involved," she said. "I apologize for being such a pain and didn't mean those snarky things I said. I am very thankful for everyone and everything. Far more than words can ever say."

I drew her into my arms, and this marked the survival of our first blowout. Isn't that the key in any relationship with someone you love? To forgive, to listen, to love unconditionally. To hug it out once all is said and done. Yes, Trish and I were definitely family now—even if we had to go to hell and back to discover it. No argument or difference in opinion was strong enough to tear apart what we were building between us.

Things got back to normal rather quickly after that. I only hoped they would continue to stay that way. When you have so many personalities under one roof, along with the pressures of a terminal illness at the core of the family, there were times I wondered if it could ever work. I would question if trying to make us a family was the right thing. I turned to prayer more often as the months wore on, looking to God for guidance. He orchestrated all of this. He had to know the struggles. Still, He had Trish's and my paths cross in that hospital room for a reason. He made a way for us that day when there seemed to be no way. I had to cling on to that. I may not see how to pull off certain things. I may not see all the answers, but God has our entire journey carved out in stone. Just knowing that made it healing to talk to Him.

> *I may not see all the answers, but God has our entire journey carved out in stone. Just knowing that made it healing to talk to Him.*

"Sometimes it seems even when we follow Your plan, Lord, there is something there to fight us," I prayed one night. "I ask for Your help in showing Trish we're only trying to make things better and not control things or make her feel helpless. Please let her see that we're a family now and she's loved, and safe, and a part of us. Lead us through this journey, as at times I feel lost. I can't do this without You. You're the light in the dark. Please, just show me the way. Amen."

I got home from work that next night with tired, aching feet. The kids were upstairs getting ready for bed, Dan was still working in his office, and Trish was resting and watching TV in her room. The dogs were even fast asleep on their blankets in the kitchen. The Seaman household was blissfully peaceful. I set my purse down and let my muscles relax. Hungry, I went to the pantry to grab some crackers and as I turned to close the door, I paused and turned back around. The foods that had been labeled "For Trish and Wesley's use only" now had their names crossed off, giving up complete ownership and making it an even playing field. No more separation. No more claiming of territory. Everything belonged to everyone, which for Trish was a huge step forward. Funny how that one minor little tweak to our family dynamic reduced me to tears as I sank down on a chair, crying with elation. Yet it wasn't a crazy reaction. Here was, in essence, the answer to the prayer I lifted to God the night before. If Trish was now able to let any of us help ourselves to Wesley's Kraft Macaroni & Cheese or her bag of Doritos, then she was finally allowing us further into her heart.

CHAPTER 18

Toes in the Sand

S omething awakened inside of me after Trish and I mended our little rift. I began to see how some special bonding time with all of us together had to become priority. Back in May when she was last hospitalized, we expected she had possibly a month to live at best, but here we were in July, and she was doing absolutely amazing. I didn't want to take that for granted. In the here and now, while God had blessed her with the strength and physical stamina to get out and do things, we had to start letting go of life's distractions and concentrate on building crucial memories as a new family.

Dan and I decided we'd all take a vacation to the beach in Fenwick Island, Delaware, where two of Trish's friends, George and Cindy, live. We rented a house in close proximity so they could do things together. It meant plenty of room for my brother and Jessica along with their three kids, my mom, and the newly formed Seaman gang including Wesley and Trish. We decided not to say anything until the plans were set and then let them in on the surprise.

I leaned in the doorway of Trish's room one evening anxious to spill the beans. "We've decided to take a family vacation. We thought we'd spend a week at the beach."

Her face sagged a bit. It wasn't the excited response I thought I'd get to enjoy. "Oh, that sounds nice. The beach is lovely."

I waited a beat. I was completely confused. "It is. We've even rented a house right near the ocean. It's only minutes away."

Again, she looked down. Not even a smile. I began to wonder if she was more of a cabin-in-the-woods type of girl. "Well, we'll watch the house for you until you get back."

Then it made sense. I'd worded it that "we" were going on a family vacation. Trish didn't realize that "we" counted them as family, too. Now was as good a time as any to make that word clear. It had certainly taken on a whole new and wonderful meaning.

"'Family' means all of us. You and Wesley are coming along. So what do you say about enjoying some fun in the sun?"

"No, Trish," I explained. "You don't understand. 'Family' means all of us. You and Wesley are coming along. So what do you say about enjoying some fun in the sun?"

Her eyes flew open as she let out a gasp. "Really? You mean all of us are going to the beach? My Lord, I had no idea. That would be so fabulous."

I laughed and nodded. "From now on, Trish, whenever you hear the word 'family,' that includes the both of you, too."

"Oh, okay. That's good. So very good. I've got so much to bring. I'd better go and start packing!"

Trish was absolutely beside herself. She hadn't been on a vacation in years because of work and never being able to afford an expensive getaway, and then, of course, her illness. But now there was nothing about to get in her way. She was packed before anybody else two weeks ahead of time. And she shopped all the way up to the day that we left. Shopped and shopped and shopped. She bought goggles and little fans that spray water if you need to cool down. Even lawn chairs that fold so she could sit in the sand. At one point, we told her that we only had so much room in the car and if she kept buying more things for the trip, we'd have to reserve a U-Haul!

On the morning we were to leave for our rental house in Bayside, a beautiful little resort community by the ocean, Trish was up at the crack of dawn. I watched her flit around the house, gathering things, checking to make sure Wesley had enough sunscreen, sand buckets, and shovels, darting from her luggage back to her closets. She was filled with adrenaline, which seemed impossible considering the sleepy side effects of her medication. I knew she packed enough outfits to last her a month and more swimsuits than I'd ever seen before. Then there was her extensive collection of wigs so she'd have different hair every day. There were long brunette tresses, short blond curls, and her favorite, an auburn bob.

"You can't go changing wigs on me once we get there, Dolly," I warned her. "I'm going to lose you down there. I won't recognize you!" We both laughed so hard we grew breathless. My teasing still didn't keep her from packing each and every one.

We went right to the beach so the kids could dip their feet in the rolling waves, but Trish grew hesitant. She couldn't walk that great a distance, and her wheelchair couldn't be pushed through the powdery sand. My brother saved the day by finding the perfect solution. At the entrance to the beach was a big white beach chair with these gigantic tires that were made to be sand-friendly for people who needed wheelchair access. Adam helped Trish get settled into it and wheeled her to the beach.

"Look at the seagulls, Wesley," she called, the wind blowing the bangs of her auburn wig from her forehead. "They're everywhere. Look at how they fly in circles."

He squinted up toward the sky. "I want to feed them, Mommy. Do we have anything? I bet they'd come real close."

"Oh, don't feed them." Trish adjusted her oversized sunglasses. "They get a little crazy and it'll be like a horror movie. Just let them be, Wesley. They are to watch, not to make friends with."

Each day we'd go out there using that same wonderful beach wheelchair, soaking up the sun, breathing in the salt air, and feeling more relaxed than we had in a very long time. The kids made sand castles, searched for seashells, and chased one another into the foam of the waves. Trish took lots of photos on her phone and sent them to Maria back in Baltimore. She particularly wanted to show her friend this new beach chair with the giant wheels that saved her whole vacation, so she asked if I'd snap a photo of her and my brother posing with it and the ocean in the background. Once I did, she sent it to Maria with the caption, "HERE'S ME AND MR. PINNACLE ON THE BEACH!" That was her nickname for Adam since he worked as a businessman for Pinnacle-Health. Not more than a minute later, Trish let out a howl and held her phone up.

"Maria likes the photo I sent. She wants to know if the man comes with the chair!"

We all shared a laugh, as now it was no secret that Maria found my married brother rather cute. He grinned and looked a little embarrassed as his cheeks began to blush.

Trish's friends Cindy and George came over two different nights and took Trish out for supper. Another night Teresa came down from Baltimore and she, Cindy, and Trish went shopping for the entire evening. It was nice because Trish could easily be pushed around in her own wheelchair on these outings since the entire development was all smoothly paved. She adored spending time with friends and being so social. I hardly ever saw her when she didn't have a smile on her face that week.

One day she and Wesley chose not to go to the beach with the rest of us; Trish wanted to go to the resort pool for a couple of hours. They needed time just for themselves. My first reaction was to panic over the thought of letting them out of my sight. There wouldn't be a responsible adult with them to watch over things and make sure Trish was okay. What if her wheelchair malfunctioned or she began not feeling well? What if she needed something and Wesley had no way to get it? Then I flashed back to the quarrel we had before she went to Baltimore where she admitted to feeling smothered and was tired of being controlled. I knew I had to be more mindful of that. I had to stop taking too much freedom away. How would I feel if I had to rely on someone to take me places when I could once just drive myself? What would I do if I always had to be watched, followed, and fussed over? Wesley was more than capable and could wheel her back to the house if necessary. It would be good for them and probably good for us, too. Those little breaks were important to everyone. Still, I made sure Trish kept her cell phone close at hand in case she needed us. As long as she had that, I had to let go and completely let God. Something that always sounds easier to do than it is. Then again, I had to get the hang of it, since this journey would only get more challenging and emotional as it continued.

On the final morning of our stay, I took Trish out in her wheelchair for one last stroll before heading home. She seemed deep in thought as she looked at all the pretty ponds, the beautiful landscape, the kids swirling around on bikes and scooters. It soothed her to take in deep breaths of sea air as she lifted her face toward the sun. Growing tired from pushing, I parked her beside a bench and sat down to rest. I was going to ask her if she had a good time but then saw a distant look in her eyes.

"What's on your mind?" I asked.

"I was just realizing how at peace I feel by the sea. I'd really like it if my ashes could be scattered at a beach somewhere. It doesn't have to be here, just anywhere where the ocean meets the sand. I think that would be perfect."

This whole trip had been so light and enjoyable that it made it easy to forget the solemn path ahead. Her profile was beautiful as she remained focused and serene, the breeze tossing her long dark hair away from her shoulders. Another wig. A different look, but always my Trish no matter what.

"I can see to it for you if you'd like," I answered, keeping my words soft and gentle.

She looked at me. "Would you? I would appreciate that."

My chest hurt right in the center. It was a kind of grief that was new to me. I had tended patients who were dying and talked with families bearing the brunt of this pain, but not someone I had grown to love. I didn't want to lose her but knew that when God needs an angel, you must let them go. She was never mine to keep, only to borrow.

CHAPTER 19

A Whole New World

After we got back from our beach vacation, it was time for our annual community carnival. It's a weeklong event with rides for the kids, games, and a fireworks display. I knew Trish would love it. True to her sassy spirit, she insisted on going every single night! She'd take Wesley with her, and I would drop them off and come back when they were ready. He played every game and bought every blowup toy they had in stock that week. Trish absolutely spoiled him in every way she could. I think in the back of her mind she knew her chances to do so were dwindling. Anything she could do, she would do.

Midweek during the carnival the fireworks show was set to take place, but the weather didn't look to be cooperating. The sky was gunmetal gray with swollen clouds moving in faster and faster. As nightfall came, the carnival decided the show must go on, but right as it was about to begin came a downpour.

"Oh, no," Trish cried, cupping her hands to her mouth. "I'm

so disappointed! I really wanted to see fireworks just one more time."

That was it. That's all it took to pit us against the elements. I wasn't about to let one monsoon keep Trish from fulfilling one of her last life's wishes.

"Let's get in the van," I said, rushing us through the rain. Once we were in, I cranked up the ignition, pulled out of the parking lot, and headed across town as fast as I possibly could. Trish and Wesley stayed silent in the back. Perhaps they wondered what had gotten into me. Finally, we reached our destination at the top of a hill where we could see every spectacular burst of color explode in the storming skies.

"Wow," Trish whispered, staring out the car windows at the breathtaking view of the fireworks above. She snuggled against Wesley, lacing her fingers with his, leaning her head on his little shoulder without making another sound. With each new blast of color, each boom, each burst of magic, she simply smiled wider. I sat back, drenched to the bone but never so content.

Once it was over and the skies grew silent and dark, I started up the engine so we could head home. Before I could move the van into reverse, I felt her edge close and give me a hug. "I really want to thank you. This meant so much to me. I just wanted to see them one more time. Just one more time. Thank you."

I let her hug me for several seconds longer than I planned. To me, that was the best part of all.

Some of my most favorite memories with Trish were when we simply spent time together. I'd be flopped on the love seat in her room as she lay in bed, the two of us watching TV, snacking, and chatting. One night, she was more into her iPad than the game show we'd been watching. She set her mouth in annoyance as she scanned a batch of emails.

"This is way off," she said almost in a huff. "I hate when well-meaning people write and say how happy they are that I found someone to care for Wesley. I didn't just find you or pick you out. You were sent to me."

> *"I didn't just find you or pick you out. You were sent to me."*

"What do you mean?" I asked.

She leaned forward, the liquid pools of her eyes soft and shining. "Tricia, when you walked into the room, I felt as though someone laid a warm blanket on me. My whole body just relaxed. I felt calm, like I couldn't describe. Somehow, at that moment I just knew."

"What did you know?"

"I knew that you were going to be there to help me. I didn't understand how or what that meant, but that you would be the one to do what needed to be done—even if I didn't realize exactly what that was at that point."

I was surprised to hear her say this. I truly had no idea she felt that way then. My insides welled as I walked over and sat on the edge of her bed, sliding my arm through hers. "Trish, I want you to know something. That warm feeling—that peace—that was God and not me. It was God's love, God's care for you. I was simply the messenger, but I am so thankful He chose me to be that messenger and so very humbled."

Even now, being too long without her, I think back to that exchange. It only confirmed even more the miracle God worked between us during my shift that night.

As July wound down, I began to notice more and more changes within myself. I always looked at life as sort of a large unknown that you pray, work, and plan for. You sink yourself 100 percent into your career, working long hours. You come home and take care of the house, tend to family, and make sure everyone has everything. You make lists, you have goals, and you make mistakes and always strive to do better tomorrow. But what if you lived like tomorrow wasn't an option? What if today was all you had? As I began to shift my way of thinking, I learned to let loose and just enjoy the moment. If things weren't exactly right, just let it be. If there were errands to run or housework to do, those things weren't going anywhere. Seeing life through Trish's eyes meant removing the blinders from my own. How many special little things had I missed because

I wasn't looking? I cringed remembering the times I chose cleaning or laundry over playing ball with the dogs, sharing a soda with one of the kids, sitting next to Dan while he watched a ballgame. Did I notice the mandarin sunset? How many times did I tune out the chime of my own children's laughter? Did I wrap my hands around a hot mug of coffee and savor the aroma, sitting back to relax, or was I in too much of a rush?

Then I would think about what I would do if I knew for sure I was going to leave this earth soon. I realized I'd do exactly what Trish was doing in her final days. I'd spend it with the people I love doing the little things that matter the most, savoring every blissful moment.

CHAPTER 20

The Birthday Kitten

One of my greatest joys was when I got to turn to a new page on my calendar in the kitchen. It meant that we had another victory. It was now August and Trish was still with us and doing pretty well, which was miraculous to everyone.

Along with the gift of more time came the chance to learn more things about Trish, including how much she adored cats. My mom has a way of having all the stray kitties in McAlisterville somehow single out her house and decide to hang around. At least, that's the version she tells, but the bag of cat food out in her garage tells the real reason she's made so many furry friends. One cat, Clementine, the stray that somehow got a name, had a litter of kittens, and Trish was enamored. She'd take Wesley there all the time, claiming he wanted to go to the pool, but in reality I think she needed her feline fix. She was the biggest cat lover I'd ever met, and was absolutely crazy for these kittens. She would pick them up and love on them, nuzzling her face deep into their fur. That was when things took a positive turn in Emma's favor.

My daughter had wanted a cat for a very long time but could never convince her dad that was a good plan. We already had our two dogs, TJ and Lily, who were a handful. We didn't even know if they'd get along with a cat, but Emma always dreamed of the day she could at least find out.

"Can't I just take one of the kittens, Dad?" Emma asked Dan one night.

"You know my answer. We've talked about this before. I just don't think we need another pet in this house."

Yet Dan slowly began to notice signs that he wasn't going to have the last say in this battle. Trish and I picked up a litter pan during one of our trips to the store along with little cat toys that began to pop up in various rooms in the house. Before my confused husband could object, Trish cornered him.

"You know, Dan, it would be like my cat, and Emma could take care of it for me."

I watched as Dan visibly softened. He absolutely could never say no to Trish. So Emma picked out one of the kittens to bring home—whether Daddy was ready for it or not. She named her Minnie after Trish's beloved cat of many years that had passed away whose photo was now displayed on our refrigerator. She was a little ball of fluff and too cute for words. Emma was in heaven. We set up Minnie's litter box and food in the basement but noticed she was doing a lot of sleeping instead of exploring. Even her new cat toys didn't capture her attention. Trish thought it was just because Minnie was so little and needed time to build up her strength. Just to be safe, we made an appointment with the vet to have her checked out the following week.

But after only two days—the morning of Emma's seventh-grade orientation—I was getting out of bed to shower and heard the most bloodcurdling scream come from downstairs. Before I could slide my robe on, Emma had already bounded up to my room.

"Mom, come quick!" she panted. "Something is wrong with Minnie. You've got to do something to help her!"

I ran down the steps to Minnie's bed and as soon as I saw her, I knew. She was on her side, completely still. The little kitten had died. Emma was inconsolable. By this time, Trish had gotten out of bed and made her way down to see what was wrong. She felt terrible. Dan hurried to get poor Minnie out of the house, so he could bury her in the backyard. Emma sat on the deck, watching her father from a distance, as she heaved and choked through sobs. I wanted to comfort her, simply to hug my hurting daughter, but as I looked out the window, I saw Trish in the chair right next to her. I leaned against the wall with the sweet late-summer air coming through the screen and listened as they talked.

"You know, Emma honey, Minnie didn't have a very long life, but what she did have you made very special for her," Trish said.

"You were the best kitty-mommy that I've ever seen anybody be. I'm sure Minnie died a happy kitten because of all the love you gave her."

I saw Emma rest her head against Trish's shoulder, nodding, quieting down, and finding solace in those precious words. As I watched the two of them, my vision blurred with tears. I would one day be mothering and comforting her son after his heart broke from her passing and here she was now, consoling my daughter, healing Emma's desperate loss and aching. Seeing this entire scene play out before me bonded me to Trish even more than I already was. I knew losing a kitten and losing a mother were two very different things, but what wasn't different was the love that comes from a mother's heart. The kind of love that is unlike any other, and Trish and I understood that. It didn't matter anymore if we were linked by blood or not. Genetics weren't in the equation. Trish and I were sharing the job of mothering our children,

Trish and I were sharing the job of mothering our children, and we made quite a dynamic duo.

and we made quite a dynamic duo.

After that tough day, Emma's birthday was just around the corner. Sadly, Minnie was part of her birthday present, which was the main reason Dan finally gave in. We weren't expecting this heartbreak, but we hoped it wasn't too late to turn that around. About a week or so later, we decided to bring home one of the last kittens still up for adoption at my mom's house. Emma was hesitant at first, unsure if she could even love another kitty the way she loved Minnie, but she named him Milo. Trish gave her stamp of approval. The two played with him nonstop. We took Milo to the vet right away, and he checked out fine, which helped put our minds at ease. The veterinarian also gave us an explanation about what could have caused Minnie to pass so unexpectedly. Being so small, her heart was most likely underdeveloped and her death would have been inevitable. Emma knew now it surely wasn't any error on her part. I think this brought her the closure she needed to fully accept and enjoy Milo. I'm delighted to say, he is still a very special part of our family.

"She's happy now," Trish commented one afternoon seeing Emma carrying Milo like a baby in her arms. "I'm so glad she was able to accept Minnie's loss and learn to love again."

I nodded in agreement, never telling Trish that I witnessed the touching moment between Emma and her on the deck that painful morning. I knew their talk was meant to be something special only the two of them shared. So I held my little secret close. Of all my memories of this woman God brought into my life, even if only for a season, that would surely be one of the most golden. One I'd never let go.

CHAPTER 21

Too Close for Comfort

M om, Megs and I are going to a late movie tonight," Anna told me rather than asked as she grabbed a juice box out of the fridge.

I sipped my tea at the kitchen island, glancing up from the magazine I was skimming. "Well, that's great, but I regret to inform you that you can't drive after midnight."

"Oh, don't worry. Trish is going along. She is going to be the adult." She stabbed the little straw into the box and eyed me as she took several gulps.

I fell back against my chair completely aghast. "Do you know how much medication Trish is on? How is she going to stay awake for that?"

"She doesn't know if she's going to stay awake or not, but she said she wants to go with us."

Who was I to argue? Anna and her friend needed a chaperone

over the age of twenty-one and they found someone to fit the bill. I surrendered and went back to reading.

That night Anna and Megs cranked up the Blazer with Trish, the designated chaperone, in the back. Off they went to the theater to see a sad movie. Just when the drama peaked, Trish fell asleep with her head thrown straight back, snoring like a beer-bellied truck driver. The girls dissolved into fits of laughter as the film reached another sad scene. Trish remained oblivious and snored even louder.

"Hey, Trish," Anna said, nudging her gently to rouse her. "You're missing the movie."

She licked her lips and rolled open her eyes, temporarily confused by her surroundings. "I'm having the most wonderful time," she drawled before nodding back off to sleep.

The girls said they couldn't stop their giggling until they finally got back home at two in the morning, where Trish could then snore in her own bed.

There were times when I felt like I was living in a circus, never knowing what was going to happen next. One day Trish decided she needed more stuff from the warehouse, so she and I made the trip. Once we arrived, I got a little squeamish. This storage shed was not my favorite place to poke around in.

"I don't typically go in this warehouse, Trish. I'm kind of scared. There's snakes."

She kept barreling ahead, wanting to get inside. "We'll be okay. Let's just try it."

I slowly approached, dreading opening the door. It made me feel worse as Trish pushed me a bit closer, impatient and wanting to get in.

"I'm going, I'm going," I said, shrugging her away. But as soon as I opened the door, my creepy crawly worst fears came true. There on the floor a mere two feet away was a snakeskin. I let loose an ear-piercing scream.

"Stop it," Trish scolded. "I've got to get in there. Can't we just look around? I'm missing my *True Blood* series collection of videos and I really want to find them."

"I told you I don't do snakes. Look at that! They're in there!"

"We're going in."

"Not me."

She put a hand on her hip. "Really? If I'm terminally ill and I'm brave enough to go in here, surely you can."

I was ready to blow my top. She had a valid point, and I didn't like it. It left me with no choice but to back down and go into the shed of horrors. So I grabbed a rake lying there to use the handle like a long pole for protection as we made our way to the back wall. If I saw so much as a caterpillar, I was ready to use my weapon. Trish searched for her videos while I kept watch for wayward reptiles. What I didn't bargain for was a huge black bat that came out of nowhere and flew over us!

I shrieked so loudly it rattled my tonsils as I threw the rake down and ran. Only once I was standing outside at a safe distance did I turn around to see Trish shaking her head, still in the same spot, cool as a cucumber.

She gave up her search and soon came out and stood alongside me. "Some help you are," she teased. "I can see the headlines now: 'Terminally Ill Woman Dies from a Rattlesnake Bite in a Warehouse, Left for Dead by Her Nurse, Who Didn't Care to Stay with Her Patient.'"

"You know I'm scared of all things that crawl. I don't do bats. I don't do snakes. You'll have to bring Dan over here if you want your DVDs."

And that's exactly what she did. With Dan's help, she got more stuff to bring back to the house.

We'd gotten through the summer with Wesley staying up all night and doing his own thing, but the first day of school was fast approaching and Dan and I knew we had to do something. We called Pastor Joe for help. We knew he'd help us talk about this with Trish in a way that was supportive and loving.

Joe came over, and we broached the subject by reminding Trish the bunk bed up in the boys' room was still empty and how when school started we wanted to get Wesley to sleep in his bed. That was very hard for Trish. She crossed her arms and began to bounce her leg up and down, a clear sign she was not wanting to consent.

"It's truly best for him," I tried to reason. "He needs a set bedtime and to get on a better eating schedule so his meals are healthier and don't consist of just snacks on the run. We can't parent him later on like we do our other kids if he doesn't learn how to follow rules."

Trish wanted what was best for her son. Letting go of some of the old routines they had kept up for so many years was imperative to paving the way for his future in our family. So she agreed.

The first night we tried to get him to sleep in his own bed was a long one. Trish explained to Wesley that things would be a bit different and he would now be sleeping in his bunk bed with Noah. We kept things calm. I did as I always did, tucking in Noah on the upper bunk. But then I went down and tucked Wesley in with Trish standing behind me, fighting off tears. Wesley began crying and grabbing for his mom, his little face red and distorted with anguish, but I stayed strong. This transition needed to happen. Eventually, he grew tired and realized no amount of bawling or begging was going to change the situation. He settled down, but I left the room feeling like the bad guy. Still, I knew in my heart that one day soon, Trish was going to get worse. When she got really sick, it would be even harder to take him out of her bed and force him into another. I couldn't one day say to him that he couldn't sleep next to his mother because she was dying and in too much pain. This needed to come from her. Trish had to tell him just where he'd be sleeping from now on. I also understood why Wesley wanted to sleep with his mom and was making this difficult. Every moment between them was treasured. So we came to a compromise that seemed to please everyone. Wesley slept in his own bed during the week, and on weekends, he could go down and sleep with his mother so they still had time together. Even with that plan in place, there were weeknights when Wesley would cry out, "Mommy, Mommy, Mommy! Don't leave me!" Dan and I would stand outside the door and just lean on each other and weep.

"I feel like my heart's just been ripped out of my chest," Trish told me in the kitchen after one of Wesley's crying sessions.

"I know," I answered, feeling raw inside, too. "But you've got to think about what's best for him. He'll be better off this way. It's something he has to learn to do."

She drew in a breath and slumped in surrender. This was essentially their first big step toward separation.

CHAPTER 22

Broadway Bound

In mid-August, God had quite a surprise for Trish. One night, late in the evening, Anna got a message from a teacher who runs the theater program at her school. There was a scheduled chartered bus trip the next day to New York City to see the Broadway show *Cinderella*. The message mentioned that the teacher's wife was ill and they both wouldn't be able to go. He asked Anna if she would like to invite Emma and an extra friend to take their places. Emma was ecstatic, which was well and good, but that still left one more opening.

"Would it be okay if I asked Trish to go?" said Anna, pleading with her eyes.

My initial response was hesitance since I had to work the following afternoon. I had never sent Trish on a trip anywhere without me, other than the beginning of the summer with Maria.

"You understand that this will be a lot of responsibility for you," I warned. "She can't walk long distances, so you'll have to take the wheelchair. Then you'll have to keep an eye on her and make sure she takes her pills."

"I want to do this," she said. "I can handle it. She'd love it."

I can still hear Trish's shrieks of excitement when I told Anna to go ahead and invite her. But as I helped Trish pack up her things, we found she didn't have enough medication to last until the next night.

"I wish we would have known so we could have refilled your pills," I said, counting the remaining batch. "This isn't enough to get you through until you get back."

Trish looked devastated. "Don't you think it will be okay if I just miss a couple?"

"You can't go past your three-hour mark, Dolly. You wouldn't be able to bear the pain."

She wanted to go so badly. How she loved an adventure and the hustle and bustle of New York City, not to mention the experience of a Broadway show. My insides felt shredded to see the look of dismay in her eyes. She'd already laid out her outfit, was choosing just the right wig, and had gathered her things with such enthusiasm. I hadn't seen her that energetic in a while. I couldn't have this all fall through. That's when I came up with a plan.

Now, let me tell you a bit more about our little community in McAlisterville. Nothing is ever too much or impossible to track down in your hour of need. I got the idea to call our pharmacist, who lived a short distance away. It was after eleven that night, but once I explained the situation, he agreed to meet me at the drive-through window with the meds that would save the day. I drove in my Pjs up to the window that had the bars pulled down after hours and on the other side was this dear man, in his sweatpants and lounging shirt. He handed me Trish's meds with a friendly wink. I will always consider him my hero even if he thinks it was only a small favor.

In the morning, I had Trish and the girls at the bus pickup by six. Jessica and my mom were going to the show, too. They both seemed shocked to see Trish.

"Tricia, what are you thinking?" my mom whispered with a glare. "This isn't a good idea."

"Mom, what am I supposed to do? She's dying. She wants to go to a Broadway show."

"What do we do if something happens to her?"

"Take her to a hospital and give me a call. You just do what is reasonable, and if I have to come there, that's what I'll do. I just can't deny her this opportunity."

As it turned out, Trish did just fine. She was provided a transport wheelchair, which had smaller wheels than the one she was used to. This made it more difficult to maneuver, especially in a city where taxis are zooming around and the sidewalks are crowded. My sister-in-law ended up pushing Trish most of the day. When they arrived at the theater, there were no elevators, so Trish had to walk up several flights of stairs, but she didn't let that stop her. She just held on to the banister and kept her eye on the prize—a seat in a Broadway theater. She loved every moment of the show, even getting to meet the cast and taking part in an acting class, too. It was a fabulous but very long day. By the time they got home, Anna admitted that the experience gave her a whole new appreciation of what her dad and I were going through. She understood now just how much work it was every time we took Trish places. But one thing was certain: she loved Trish as much as we did. For my sweet daughter, nothing else mattered as long as Trish had a day to remember.

Since the summer was winding down, we decided to make a jaunt out to Knoebels, an amusement park about forty-five minutes away. The family went for the day and it was fun, but a challenge. The park wasn't paved and had little stones underfoot, so pushing Trish's wheelchair was taxing.

> *Trish had a blast and rode every ride she could. Sometimes it was hard to tell just who was the kid— Trish or Wesley.*

I'll never forget watching her and Wesley on the giant Ferris wheel. It was so big and so high, I swear, if they reached their hands in the air, it looked like they'd be touching the clouds. Trish had a blast and rode every ride she could. Sometimes it was hard to tell just who was the kid—Trish or Wesley.

I learned something new about Trish that day. She adored carousel horses. She bought one that afternoon at a souvenir shop.

"I've always loved them," she admitted. "I have an entire collection of beautiful carousel horses that we packed away in one of my boxes in your basement. I've never really been able to admire and enjoy them as much as I'd like."

"Why not?" I noticed a touch of regret in her gaze.

"I was younger when I collected them. It was before Wesley was born, so once he got to be a toddler, I wrapped each one and stored them in the garage. I didn't want him to break them, and I didn't have a curio cabinet or anywhere to display them. I guess life got in the way."

Her last remark stuck with me. If life gets in the way, there are times you have to plow right through it. In this case, I wanted Trish to enjoy her beloved carousel horses while there was still time. Once we got home, I went to the basement and I unpacked each one, wiping them off, making them shine, bringing them up, and setting them around her in her bedroom where she could finally appreciate them.

"I'd forgotten how magnificent they all are," she said misty-eyed, scanning her treasures. "I can't thank you enough for doing this. They are gorgeous."

I took a moment and admired them with her. I wasn't sure, though, what was more beautiful—the collection of horses or the splendor on my friend's face. It's a look I still remember.

As the month of August progressed, I noticed Trish's energy level was beginning to decline. She wasn't doing as much running around, and sometimes she complained about feeling tired. She was getting confused when trying to remember the proper dosages of her medications. Luckily, she had a personal nurse at her disposal. I took all the narcotics and put them in a lockbox where I knew she couldn't slip up and accidentally overdose. The move relieved my mind in one way, yet tortured it in another. She was beginning to lose the battle. Loss of energy was the first of many signs that would soon follow. My gut felt like a knotted rope.

One day I came home from work and went right to her room to check on her. She was trying frantically to clean up her bathroom where it seemed the toilet had overflowed. When I took a closer look, an entire bottle of liquid foundation had also been dumped into the mess.

"I'm not sure what happened," she said with remorse and a twinge of embarrassment. "I went to the bathroom and I flushed the toilet, but maybe I flushed it one too many times."

I assured her it was okay and told her to let me take care of it. I could tell she felt bad, since I'd just come home from a long shift. When I was done, I went back and sat beside her. She looked at me so defeated.

"I'm sorry, Tricia. I cause you so much work."

"It's fine," I insisted. "A little Clorox and it's all cleaned up."

She hung her head, and I put my arm around her. This was a

genuine moment between the two of us. I honestly didn't mind helping, despite my sore feet and aching back—Trish had begun to feel like family and I loved her. She had mellowed me. Things didn't get under my skin quite as easily as before. This was minor compared to what she was facing. I would do anything for her, but the problem was, the one thing she needed most wasn't in my power to give.

CHAPTER 23

Steps Toward Heaven

PinnacleHealth had been supportive of us from day one and wanted us to have something—an outlet to share our story, as well as to post it on YouTube and the hospital's website for others to see. I began to worry that we had waited too long since we were noticing more and more signs of Trish's condition deteriorating. If we were going to have a video capturing Trish's legacy to keep and to share, it was now or never. So, on August 29, 2014, a film crew came to our home and filmed *Tricia and Tricia: A Family Story*. It came out so beautifully, and both Trish and I were proud to share it and have for our own personal enjoyment.

Not long after the video was posted, Kelly McCall, the public relations contact at the hospital, called us to say that she was good friends with Kendra Nichols from our local ABC affiliate and to ask if she could pass along the link to her. Trish and I agreed, not expecting anything from it, but to our surprise, the crew from ABC came out and did an interview for television. From there, our story appeared on the web and in local newspapers. Letters began to pour in from people touched and inspired, offering prayers for Trish and my family. This support meant so much to Trish—she read every single letter that came. We began to realize that our story could actually make a difference. Trish sat me down and made me promise her one thing: no matter what happened, I needed to keep sharing our story—even after she was gone.

Oftentimes, Trish would come to me needing to talk about what was waiting for her on the other side. It's common to wonder and imagine what happens to us after we die. Descriptions in the Scriptures and Bible stories offer a preview, but her questions were urgent. She needed answers now, as she would be making that transition soon.

"Do you think that I'll be able to see my son and watch him grow up in heaven? Will I be able to see what you are all doing?"

I wanted to give her my honest, true feelings. She deserved nothing less.

These conversations were difficult to have. I thought for a moment, not wanting to pacify my friend by telling her what I thought she wanted to hear. I wanted to give her my honest, true feelings. She deserved nothing less.

"You know, the Bible tells us a few very clear things—like when you become absent from the body, you're present with the Lord. It tells us there are streets of gold in heaven and once we see Jesus, we're so consumed with praising Him that we don't think about much else. I think time is different in heaven than it is here. Many years on Earth may seem like a blink of an eye up there. That's what I believe."

"Do you think I'll see my parents? Will they be there when I go?"

It was hard to respond. In truth, I didn't have the answers and had to go with my heart.

"I think if your loved ones who had gone on before you knew God, which you said that many of them did, then you will see them again."

"Hmm," Trish said, seemingly satisfied judging from the soft curve of her lips.

Wesley had challenges of his own as we continued through this ordeal. It was confusing, since his mother and I had such different parenting styles, often leaving him caught in the middle. I was the one always coming behind saying, "Absolutely not. We're not doing that." I was the taskmaster. I was the person who set limits, while essentially his mother had none. But he liked me and adjusted to two different sets of parenting techniques: Tricia's rules and Mommy's rules. I know this was hard for him. He wanted to fit in with us, but he also loved doing it Mommy's way because there were no boundaries. I also knew and could understand that Trish was trying to live every last moment with him and often spoiled him while she still could more than she ever did before. She knew she was dying, and all she wanted before her life slid away was to see her son happy. I didn't step in too much because I understood her. There would come a time when it would be in my hands. I knew from the past, Wesley adjusted well to the Seaman way of doing things. But for now I hung back to let the two of them be true to themselves. Trish was still here in the flesh. She was still his mother and for that, I was so very thankful.

By the time school started in late August, Trish declared to me one day, "I think I've bought just about everything I can think of buying from Walmart. I have enough clothes for Wesley and I have stuff for myself that I'm probably going to die before I ever get a chance to wear. I just don't know what to shop for anymore."

These words would've been sweet relief to me months before, but now I realized Trish's hobby was a motivation for her. I honestly feared that if she couldn't have the joy of shopping, we might lose her sooner. She needed as many reasons to keep pressing on as possible and that included spending her disability check.

"Why not shop for things for Wesley for the future?" I replied. I didn't plan to say it, yet I felt it deep inside where God whispers. To this day, I believe it was He leading her in a special direction.

"What do you mean?" She cocked her head.

"Maybe start buying sentimental items I can give to him from you at times you may no longer be with us, like birthdays and Christmas. It would be so meaningful to him, I'm sure."

Well, that gave her a whole new quest. Her shopping went into overdrive. She bought tons of clothes for Wesley in larger sizes for the coming years when he grew up. Winter clothes, summer clothes, snow jackets, gloves in all sizes from boyhood to young man. For the birthdays she would miss, she thought ahead to when he'd turn sixteen and ordered a keychain engraved with a loving message saying, "Drive safely. Love, Mom." She bought him a money clip and wallet for his graduation from high school with a note to save his money. I was witnessing my friend experience the stages of grief. She seemed so angry and upset when she first came to live with us and was often not accepting of her reality. Now she embraced the actuality of what was happening and was preparing wisely. She knew she was dying, and she was going to meet it head on with nothing left unfinished.

Around this time, Trish would often sit on the couch in the front room and listen to my daughters whenever they would play the piano and sing together. Trish loved the sound of their voices. It brought her a sense of peace. Only later did I learn that Trish had approached Anna to help put music to a song that she'd been writing for me. Trish had the words but needed my daughter to take to the piano and give it a melody. She had been moved to tears a few weeks ago, when I dedicated and sang "You're Not Alone" by Meredith Andrews at church and wanted to do the same for me. It was important to her to keep it a secret—her goal was to finish the song so that Anna could sing it to me at Trish's funeral. The two worked together on it every time I wasn't home. It was her way of taking a step in truly accepting her fate and wanting to leave a piece of her heart behind to give comfort when she passed.

Trish and I rarely had moments when it was just the two of us alone. After all, we shared a busy home with five children! So it was special the day when I took her to eat Chinese food while Dan watched the kids. We took our time—laughing and talking. She shared some rather colorful war stories from her wild dating days.

And then she paused and asked, "What was your life like before you met Dan?"

"I went to church and college," I answered. A flush traveled up my cheeks.

"That's all you've got? You went to church and college?"

"Boring, huh?"

She began to object to make me feel better but decided there was no use in pretending.

"That's about as boring as watching paint dry!"

We laughed so hard together that day that the other diners in the restaurant began to glance over at us. Trish and I were total opposites. Yet, amazingly, God paired us together. The talk took a serious turn as I shared how I couldn't imagine life without her there. She admitted she didn't want to leave—she loved being a part of a family. It was what she'd dreamed and hoped for, and she didn't want it ever to go away.

"Don't worry," I assured her with every ounce of my being. "It won't. Family is forever, so don't forget that."

Looking back, that kind of moment is what I miss the most with her gone. When we would just sit, have lunch or dinner, and chat about everything. It was during those times that we would have some of our best conversations. Often late at night when I was loading the dishwasher, she would shuffle out in her slippers, and we'd end up sharing a big bowl of ice cream together. She showed me how wonderful the simple things in life could be.

"I see him getting a lot closer to you," Trish said one day while we both sat on the front porch while the boys played ball in the yard. "I'm really happy for that."

I was startled. Of course, she meant Wesley, but I wasn't sure to what she was referring. I knew he liked me and we enjoyed each other, but I was still self-conscious about my role in his life.

"I see him getting a lot closer to you," Trish said one day. "I'm really happy for that."

"How?" I asked. "What have you seen?"

"You've been tending to him a lot now that I'm growing more

tired. He lets you. He's depending on you and it's nice. I'm glad he's got you," she said, never taking her gaze from her boy.

I suddenly felt warm inside as if sunlight had filled me up. "I am, too."

The first week of September, I took Trish for a CAT scan to give us a better timeline of her progression. The boys' school held an open house the next day, which was a good distraction as we waited to hear the test's results. We met the teachers—Trish loved asking them questions and seeing the classrooms and desks where her son would be learning. I noticed her getting reflective.

"He's getting so big," she said, her gaze clouded with so many thoughts and feelings. "Third grade already. Where does the time go? I wish I could slow things down."

I could only shake my head and hug her close. "I know, Dolly. I wish we could, too."

The following day after the open house, we met with Dr. Shah for the results of the CAT scan. Trish was visibly disappointed when she learned there was little change. This wasn't a surprise— we knew the cancer was relentless and she was going to die and soon. Still, I believe a part of Trish held on to hope that it would miraculously disappear.

I tried to shift the mood in the room to a more positive note, as I shared with Dr. Shah all the adventures Trish had been having, including her recent trip to New York City to see a Broadway show.

"I'm so glad to hear this," Dr. Shah said, beaming at Trish. "You've done far better than most in your condition. Whatever your secret is, keep up with it. It certainly seems to be working."

Trish glanced over at me, then looked back at her oncologist.

"There's no secret. It's what keeps all of us going: a faith in God, a wonderful family, and love."

CHAPTER 24

The Calm Before the Storm

O nce school started in September, Trish was drained of energy and slept more and more. So when we heard a bit of exciting news, the timing was more than perfect. After Pinnacle made the video of our story, we learned that several anonymous benefactors wanted to do something special for Trish—to make a dream come true while she still had a chance to enjoy it. At first, I remembered she told me she'd love to go to Disney World, but I was concerned how well she'd travel on the long trip to Florida. Then it occurred to me. I pictured Trish's beloved Randy from the TLC bridal show in his fancy suit a mere four hours away.

"I've got it," I exclaimed. "She'd absolutely love to go to New York City to Kleinfeld Bridal where they tape the show *Say Yes to the Dress!*"

This was the perfect idea for her, and I'll never forget her reaction as she bounced up and down like a kangaroo. She'd been so sick lately and quickly losing steam that it was so nice to see her excited about something.

"Is this for real? I'm going to Kleinfeld? You wouldn't tease me about this, Tricia. This would be the ultimate. Are you sure? I mean, are you really sure?"

On September 12, Robbin, Trish, and I traveled in a luxury car to New York City. Our chauffeur was an adorable elderly man named Gene, who ran the streets of the Big Apple like nobody's business. He zipped and zagged until we got to the curb right in front of the Kleinfeld Bridal showroom. From there, Trish sort of floated in. I think one of us should have pinched her.

We checked in as if we had an appointment. We weren't sure how much time they'd give us and figured we'd most likely see a tour of the bridal store. But when the consultant came out, she treated us like real customers looking to purchase an expensive wedding gown. I decided I needed to pull her aside.

"I know you work on commission, so I think I need to clear something up," I explained. "I don't want to waste your time—do you know why we're really here? Do you know who we are?"

She smiled warmly. "Oh, honey . . . we know. We all read the letter that Pinnacle sent to us. Believe me, everyone here knows."

To our surprise, Trish was given the entire Kleinfeld experience, starting with sitting in the consultant's room sharing her journey of living with cancer, which moved everyone to tears. The next thing we knew, there was a knock at the door. Trish nearly fainted when in walked none other than Randy.

"Oh, Randy!" she shrieked. "Oh, my gosh. Are you real? I'm so glad you came!"

"Nice to meet you, sweet thing! Today is your day." He moved with the same grace and expressed the same flamboyant personality as he shows on television.

Once Trish caught her breath and reclaimed her bearings, she introduced Robbin and me. Bursting into tears wasn't something I planned on, but that's exactly what I did! As soon as the waterworks started, Randy fluttered right over to me.

"Now, darlin', why are you crying?" he asked.

I blushed with embarrassment but felt like I was literally bubbling over. "It's just that meeting you is her dream come true," I said with a sniffle.

"It's just that meeting you is her dream come true," I said with a sniffle.

He patted my shoulder and flipped a neatly folded paper tissue out of his lapel pocket. I wiped my eyes, but before I could mop up my nostrils, Trish jumped a mile ready to grab the prized possession from my hands.

"Don't you dare blow your nose on that," she scolded. "Save it! You have to save it!"

I knew Trish thought it was the ultimate souvenir, so I slipped it into my purse.

They gave us the grand tour of the famous store and allowed Trish to try on some of their beautiful wedding dresses. I could tell she felt like a princess in the gowns of silk, satin, and tulle, with pearls, sequins, and rhinestones—she sparkled like the night sky. Once she found the gown she loved the best—the one with the highest price tag and the most bling—then she had the magical moment during every show when the consultant and Randy asked the famous question.

"Trish," they chimed in together, "are you saying yes to the dress?"

"Yes!" she exclaimed.

By the time we left, she had met the owners, all the consultants she knew by name from the show, and even had a little gift bag filled with luxury soaps wrapped in silver foil, a Kleinfeld mug, and everyone's business card. Trish cherished each thing, especially the mug where Randy's tissue was tucked inside. She kept it proudly on display on her bed table like the Hope Diamond in the Smithsonian right up until her dying day.

From there, we went to Ellen's Stardust Diner, where they sing Broadway tunes to you the entire time you eat. Trish had heard of it and wanted so badly to stop in. She loved Broadway and everything about it. We then headed home. It had been quite a day. The kind that felt so perfect, you think it must have been a dream.

Two days later, our family took a second trip also made possible by anonymous donors. This time a limo picked us up and we traveled to Philadelphia to the Lego Brick Fest and the King of Prussia Mall. The girls would certainly enjoy the shopping spree, but Trish really wanted to have this grand experience at the Lego Fest with Wesley since she knew it would be a memory he could hold on to. Being surrounded by Legos as far as his little eyes could see would be his dream come true. She didn't want to miss seeing his expression. It was a very special outing for the two of them.

Our family had a wonderful afternoon. By the end of the day when it was time to return home, Trish was completely drained. She was still able to walk at this point in her illness, but she tired easily. I realized that this would most likely be the last weekend she would be able to be so active. I was just so happy it had been everything she had hoped for and more. I still don't know who the anonymous donors were who made those two trips possible. My only prayer is that somehow they know that they made Trish the happiest she'd ever been.

As September came and the air grew crisp with fall, Trish's health started going downhill quickly. She lost her appetite and started sleeping for large parts of the day. I would try to wake her to entice her to eat something, but as she grew more and more disinterested in food, I knew we weren't moving in a good direction.

My birthday is in the first week of October, and Trish rose to the occasion, pulling herself out of her lethargy to celebrate. My family presented me with a cake and lovely gifts, but I was most touched by Trish's present. Earlier in the summer, Trish bought herself a silver cross necklace that hung on a delicate silver chain. I loved how it looked and often complimented her when she wore it. For my birthday, she surprised me with the exact same necklace. It touched me so deeply that with everything she was going through, she would even remember to buy me a gift. Especially something so special just between us that would be that meaningful connection I would need to feel close to her even after she was gone.

While Trish somehow held strong for my birthday festivities, the following week her condition completely crashed and she was in bed all the time suffering unbearable pain. On Wednesday morning, when I came down to check on her before I left for work, I found her sitting up and curled over, clutching her stomach, her face as white as a sheet.

"Honey, what's wrong?" I asked, noting she was sweating profusely.

"I don't know. I'm just having so much pain. I've been throwing up and used the trashcan. I just can't make it back and forth to the bathroom anymore."

I quickly set up the portable potty next to her bed along with a bucket so she wouldn't have to get up and down. The whole while I did so, my pulse began to jackhammer.

I called out of work, then anxiously waited for the clock to reach 8:00 a.m. so I could see the kids off to school and call hospice to have our nurse, Chrissy, come and check on her.

"We'll have to get some IV pain medicine started right away," Chrissy said as soon as she arrived. Trish wasn't in favor of this at all. To her this was a sign she was getting closer to dying. She refused to stop fighting. It took Chrissy and I encouraging her that this medicine was the same she'd been taking in pill form, only in higher concentrations to make her more comfortable. Our explanation must have eased her concerns as she sank back against her pillows and gave in.

The IV would be in a little shoulder bag so Trish could still move about and be functional. I knew this would calm her down, but I also knew she was deteriorating quickly. She certainly wouldn't be able to be active and do things like she wanted, as she could barely get out of bed at this point. Her condition only worsened as the week progressed. The medicine wasn't working well anymore— the pain never seemed to ease no matter what we tried. The only thing Trish could do was endure it. My mom came over one evening that weekend and for the first time in days, Trish walked out of her bedroom. My sweet friend moved gingerly to the kitchen counter carrying her little bag with the IV pump. She was pale, horribly feeble, grimacing with every step. She started to cry from places deep and aching, realizing the cancer was finally winning.

I went over to her and tried to be the strength that she needed even though I felt like I was dying alongside her. "Hey, Dolly. It's good to see you standing up. How about something to eat or maybe a milkshake?"

She hadn't had anything to eat or drink all day. Her nightgown hung on her emaciated frame.

"Maybe later on," she said. "It sounds good, but I'm just not hungry right now. Maybe later on."

I believed my nursing career had prepared me in every way to deal with the end of life. I had seen patients I cared for and their families grapple for strength when things took a turn for the worse, and I offered compassion, clean sheets, a full pitcher of water, and smiles to ease the suffering. Yet as Trish turned back and carried her pump like an old purse in her hand, she was fading away before me, and I felt such a helplessness I'd never known before. Death was invading our home, taking over the fun times, the great meals we shared, the joyful outings with the kids. It was cruel and unfeeling. Worst of all, it would soon shatter our world.

"Dear Lord, we're losing her," I later prayed once the house grew dark and still. "We love her so much, how do we let her go? I know she'll be happy, whole, and healthy in Your presence in heaven, but please . . . as selfish as it is, please . . . I'm begging You . . . for more time."

I spent the night downstairs on the love seat near her bed. I didn't know how close we were to the end. Now that she had the IV, she could press the button to dispense extra doses of pain medication. We set an alarm to go off at intervals all night, pushing the button for temporary relief, but she remained miserable. Anger raged inside of me that I couldn't do anything to make her better. All I could do was lie there so she didn't feel alone.

By that next day, I knew we needed to do something. I didn't want Wesley or my children to see her decline any further. We tried to shelter them from what was going on as much as was reasonably possible. So far, between school and Dan taking them out to eat and to the movies, they hadn't been exposed to the reality of the situation. All we told them was that Trish was needing the IV and extra bed rest to regain her energy. I called Chrissy again and our social worker Pam to let them know that things had gotten serious and the medicine was no longer easing Trish's suffering. By the time they arrived at my house, Trish had finally fallen asleep, allowing the three of us women time to share a cup of coffee and talk quietly in the kitchen.

As we sat at the island, Pam and Chrissy looked at me with remorse and sadness. Chrissy was the first one to speak—uttering the two words that crumbled my composure.

"It's time," she said firmly.

I clutched my cup with both hands, squeezing it so hard that I thought it might burst, and then I dissolved into tears.

"I can't imagine letting her leave here, but I can't take care of her anymore. What do I do? She's been such a gift in my life. I don't know how to let her go."

Pam grabbed a napkin from the counter so I could dab my tears. "It's time to move her onward, Tricia. You can't do this anymore. You've got your family to take care of and a job that needs you. You don't have the ability to keep her comfortable any longer and monitor her meds. She needs a place where nurses can tend to her twenty-four hours a day." She paused a moment. "Do you want to tell her or would you rather I talk to her and let her know?"

I drew a breath and fought for strength. There was no time to fall apart. My focus switched from my own needs and fears to what was best for the woman I dearly loved.

"I'll tell her."

I stood and summoned all of the courage I could. Then I walked into Trish's room.

CHAPTER 25

Letting Go

The clutter that once was enough to make me cringe was now so very endearing. All of her things reflected a part of herself, a reflection of her personality, as well as bits and pieces of happy memories. I reached out and held one of her carousel horse snow globes, throbbing inside to be able to turn back time and relive that day at the amusement park. Leveling my gaze to where Trish lay sleeping, I gently lowered myself to the side of her bed. I fumbled for her fragile hand, holding it in between mine like a butterfly I didn't want to set free.

She batted her eyes open and focused on me. "How are you feeling, Dolly?" I asked.

"Oh, I'm just trying to sleep in between the waves of pain."

I shifted a bit, but there was no comfortable position. "Honey, I think we've gotten to the point now that it's time. It's time."

At this news, she got very alert—her eyes now perfectly round instead of groggy slits.

"No! No! I don't want to. I think I'm going to be okay. Please, I can't. I've got outfits ready for church that I need to wear."

Through our grief, in that bittersweet moment, we both paused to laugh. She had outfits already planned, yet she couldn't even get out of bed to use the bathroom. It was a bit of the old Trish trying to come back to the surface, but this time the spark just wasn't strong enough.

"Trish, when you first came here, we both agreed that when it got to the place where I would have to be with you all the time, we'd look at going back to the hospital where they can take care of you better than I can."

> *Her tears soaked her pillowcase. "Nobody can take care of me better than you."*

Her tears soaked her pillowcase. "Nobody can take care of me better than you."

It felt as if a fist had punched through my breastbone and ripped my heart from my chest. "I will always be with you, no matter what. Always."

Her chin trembled. "I love it here."

"We love having you here, but not like this; we can't get you comfortable. I just don't have the tools here to do that."

"I know," she said, barely audible now. "I really do. I know."

Chrissy and Pam put a plan into motion. An ambulance would come to take her to the hospital, and the medical supply company would arrive later in the day to remove the equipment from the house. I called the school and arranged for the kids to take the bus home to my mom's house for the afternoon. I didn't want Wesley to come back and find his mother gone and her room empty.

Chrissy and Pam had been my mountain of strength and were just as concerned about me as they were about Trish. Before they left, Pam embraced me. "I know it's hard, but it's time to let somebody else take over. You did all that you could."

I hugged her back, leaning against her as I felt as if I might fold.

I pulled myself together, and then Trish and I started packing up some things for her to take with her to the hospital. She wanted her iPad, toiletry items, some clothing, and her wigs. She only wanted her stylish tresses near as a source of comfort—a part of her she wasn't ready to let go of yet.

It was then that I spotted her silver cross necklace on the dresser. I picked it up and walked over to her. "Do you want your necklace?"

She thought for a bit as her eyes grew misty. "No. I want you to have it."

I took mine off, removed the little cross from the chain, and then slid it onto hers so that they hung together as a perfect pair. I then put both necklaces on—they represented a symbol of eternal love and connection.

"Now they'll always be together," I said, touching the two crosses and seeing her smile. "They'll never ever be apart."

I packed up her Bible and a few more things that I would bring over to the hospital with me. I also called Dan to let him know all that happened and that I'd pick the kids up later on so I could have a chance to tell Wesley. We said a quick prayer on the phone before we hung up. He loved Trish, too, and was hurting right along with me. Jessica came over and picked me up after Trish had been transported ahead of us. I called en route and spoke to Arlene, who was going to be Trish's doctor once she was admitted to the hospital. It was no longer about needing an oncologist. It was no longer about needing a medical doctor. It was now about needing Dr. Bobonich, who was going to be able to keep Trish from suffering as she had been. Arlene met

> *"Now they'll always be together," I said, touching the two crosses and seeing her smile. "They'll never ever be apart."*

us at the emergency room to go over the details. Working her magic, she was able to get Trish's pain under control—she could finally get some rest. As fate would have it, she was back in Room 173—the same room where our whole journey began. This was no coincidence. I knew God put her there for a reason and it was confirmation that I was doing the best thing for my friend.

When I walked into that room again, my insides surged with emotion. So much had transpired since that first time. I couldn't resist reliving a bit of the past but adding a twist of the present.

"Hi, I'm Tricia," I announced. "And I'm not going to be your nurse today. I'm going to be your family forever and ever."

Trish broke into a grin. A glimmer of light in the storm. We had come a long way since I first wrote my name on her whiteboard.

That night was the big homecoming football game and dance at the high school. Anna was a homecoming candidate, so she had organized all the girls to come to the house so Trish could see everybody dressed up, but now that wasn't going to happen. Trish tried to hide her disappointment and told us to take plenty of pictures for her to see. But before I went home to get ready for the evening, I had a special little boy I had to talk with.

I went to my mom's house after school and intercepted Wesley to tell him his mommy had to be taken to the hospital and that we couldn't fix her pain anymore at our house. He seemed to handle it well, but I noticed I was now the one he clung to—he became my Velcro child. At the football game that night, he practically sat in my lap. If he couldn't have Mommy, I was the next best thing. It was our first transition from Wesley being in the middle of two moms to him having just me. I prayed I was ready for this.

Over the summer, Trish's brother, Ollie, and his wife, Erin, had moved to Florida after Erin got a new job. I made a point to call the next day and let him know all that had happened with Trish. He was such a comfort and agreed that we did the right thing for his sister. The girls from Baltimore were also contacted and made an immediate trip to spend time with Trish. The meds were heavy, and she was incoherent, sleeping most of the time and confused when she was awake, not making much sense and rambling. Still, on some level she seemed to know her support group was there as she reached out to hold their hands.

On Sunday, I went to the hospital with one mission in mind. It had been too long since Trish had been able to stand or function, so I wanted to give her a sponge bath. It was something I could still do to help her to feel better. Even if I could no longer take care of her at home, I knew she'd love the soothing feel of the warm water, feeling clean, and having me there to pamper her. With the aid of my nursing friend Kristin, who was working that day, we got a pan of water and began to sponge her down.

"What are you doing to me?" Trish asked, finally alert for the first time in days. "Just let me get up and take a shower."

I held her shoulders as she was trying to sit. "Honey, we can't even get you out of bed and into the shower the way things are. You can't even stand. We're just trying to wash you and freshen you up a bit."

She may have been near death's door, but after she was dry and in a fresh hospital gown, her fiery spirit still shone through.

"You know, Tricia, everybody around here just raves about how you give such a nice bath, but I'm here to tell you that it was cold and I didn't enjoy it," she joked.

While Trish remained in the hospital, I tried to cling to some kind of normalcy, for my own sake and for my family at home. I kept on working normal hours, Jenna held her sweet-sixteen birthday party at my brother's barn, and at the end of October, the kids went trick-or-treating. Dan was my hero for holding down the fort and entertaining the kids while I spent long hours visiting Trish.

One gray morning, I stopped into my boss's office, slumped in a chair beside her desk, and released a heavy sigh.

"I never knew it would be this hard," I told her. "I'm not sure how this is all going to work. I might need some time off now that things are . . ." I couldn't quite finish my thought.

Jackie stared back with empathy and understanding. "Tricia, anything you need. Anything at all. You just let us know."

I expressed my appreciation, but there was nothing that anyone could do—I needed my dear friend back. I wanted more time.

In early November, Trish was transported from the hospital to a hospice residence in Harrisburg. It wasn't anything like we expected. In fact, it was a house in a beautiful wooded area. It felt welcoming as soon as you pulled into the parking area. When I first walked into Trish's room, she seemed so much happier.

"Now, this is what I'm talking about," she stated. "This is where I need to be. If I can't be at your house, this is the next best thing."

And it was. It was so homey and didn't look or smell like a medical facility, let alone a place where people come to live out their final days. It had a kitchen, a living room, and a dining room. Pretty flowers were everywhere. The house could hold only seven patients, but they had nurses on staff around the clock to care for them with genuine compassion and dedication.

Trish's room was lovely, like a regular bedroom with a normal bed instead of the hospital bed. She had a dresser, a big recliner, and a TV. We tried to make it look as personal and comforting as possible, bringing photos of her and Wesley, the family, her carousel horses—even her Randy mug and his white paper handkerchief—all to remind her of our magical months together. She kept her wigs and several colorful outfits on standby in her closet. I knew her inside and out by now. Terminal or not, those gorgeous hairstyles and fashion statements were going to stay at arm's reach. Having them nearby meant something to Trish and brought her comfort.

Despite the nice location, Trish took a sharp turn for the worse after going a month barely eating or drinking. The doctors still had her on the IV pain medicine, but she kept slipping further away.

I called everyone I could think to call; time was of the essence. Trish's friends from Baltimore came up every weekend. Everyone knew it wouldn't be much longer. Emotions ran high as each day blurred into the next.

In early November, there was a parent-teacher conference for Wesley at his new school. I went to the conference but called Trish to include her. Thankfully, I caught her on a good day and she was able to take part in the meeting on speakerphone and talk to Wesley's teacher. He was doing incredibly well in school and got an excellent report card. It meant so much to Trish still to be involved in every aspect of his life—even up until the very end.

As Thanksgiving approached, I was unsure how to handle the holiday. A celebration with a big spread of food wasn't something Trish could take part in, so my family and I made the decision to stay home and surround Wesley with love, since he was unfamiliar with large family gatherings. As hard as we tried, I know we all felt Trish's absence. Wesley was quiet, not as bouncy, and clung to one of his Happy Meal toys, most likely one from a McDonald's trip with his mom. To be honest, at times my feelings of helplessness led to anger at the unfairness of it all. Did it seem too much for someone just to be able to live and enjoy her family? This was her dream. We were her dream. Why couldn't she just be here? But no matter how long we had, in truth, it would always fall short. I thought ahead to school events, Christmas, New Year's, Valentine's Day—there would never be enough time.

Like salt in a wound, Wesley's ninth birthday was November 29. Trish, of course, had planned ahead and purchased more than ten presents for him. I wrapped everything and put it in a gigantic gift bag so he could open them when he went to visit her. But for the day, I wasn't sure quite what to do. Trish and I had discussed it back during the summer, and we decided to throw him a big party at the church with all of his classmates and Sunday school friends. She had never been able to give him a big party, so we decided we were going to do it up right. This little boy was going to have quite the celebration, but now his mommy was sick and absent. The only thing I felt I could do was explain to Wesley what his mother and I planned on doing. It was important that he know she wanted the best for him on his special day.

"Wesley, we can still do a party with all of your friends if you would like to," I offered. "It's up to you. It's your birthday. Just tell me how you'd like to do this."

He lowered his chin. "I don't think I want a big party."

"And that's okay. What about doing something special with a few friends of your choice?"

And that's how we did it. He invited a couple close friends and Noah for dinner at McDonald's, his mommy's favorite. We then went to the movies and ended the night at Walmart. Somehow it seemed fitting.

On Sunday, we had cake, ice cream, and presents with my mom, Jessica and Adam, and all the kids. But when it came time for Wesley to go visit his mom so she could give him her gifts and spend time with him, it felt wrong for me to go. I didn't feel comfortable being a part of that, as if somehow I was intruding. Trish should have enjoyed taking the boys to the movies and to McDonald's, not me. My heart felt torn. On the one hand, I was glad to do those things with Wesley, but on the other hand, I was grief-stricken to know I was losing my friend and she wasn't able to take part in these celebrations. I asked my brother if he and Jessica and their kids would take Wesley down to see Trish to celebrate with her and have a little party. They were more than happy to do so and understood I wanted to make that experience about the two of them—mother and son. I sent them off with all the supplies, and they took pictures and made it a

> *I sent them off with all the supplies, and they took pictures and made it a special time for Mommy and Wesley.*

special time for Mommy and Wesley. I knew they didn't have many more chances left to share together.

CHAPTER 26

Heaven Gains an Angel

During the last couple of weeks of Trish's life, she would often text Maria and me. She was feeling so miserable and it broke my heart. One of her texts to me read: "I never thought I'd be ready to go to heaven, but I'm ready. I know everything here is okay. I know that Wesley is going to be alright. So I'm ready for God to take me now."

My eyes blurred with tears as I read her words, yet how could I blame her? She'd been kicking and fighting against her final day for months, but now it couldn't come fast enough. I even found myself praying that God would take her, too, so she could be at peace instead of going through such suffering.

Toward the last days of November, I would visit her and ask if she wanted me to read something uplifting.

"Yeah," she answered, bobbing her head a bit.

"Do you want me to read from the Bible?"

She bobbed her head again.

"What book or verse would you like to hear?"

"Your favorite ones." She closed her eyes and waited.

I turned to Philippians 4:6–7 (NKJV) and began to read. "Be anxious for nothing, but in everything by prayer and supplication, with thanksgiving, let your requests be made known to God; and the peace of God, which surpasses all understanding, will guard your hearts and minds through Christ Jesus." I completed the verse and put the Bible aside.

"That's my favorite part, too. Would you read it to me again?" Trish asked.

Sitting at her bedside, I'd repeat the scripture, and she'd soak up every word, the look on her face finally tranquil.

On December 1, I went to visit Trish after work that night. As soon as I walked in the room, she looked at me and said, "If you would lay in the bed next to me and just hold me, I think I could die."

I forced myself to breathe normally. This wasn't what I was prepared to hear.

"Okay," I answered. "I'm not sure if it works that way, but I will certainly lie next to you."

> *As soon as I walked in the room, she looked at me and said, "If you would lay in the bed next to me and just hold me, I think I could die."*

I carefully got into her bed as she lay with her back to me in a fetal position. I curled up tight around her, my arms drawing her as near as our bodies would allow, and I buried my face into the jagged bones of her spine, sobbing softly as words poured forth.

"I'm not ready for you to go," I cried.

"I know, but I'm ready."

"I just wish we could have been family our whole lives."

She burrowed tighter against me, clutching my arms wrapped around her. There was a wheeze when she went to speak.

"You will be my family from this day forward. We will always be family. Whenever I get to heaven, I'll be watching over all of you. Whenever you get there, we'll have a lot to talk about and catch up on a whole lifetime of things."

I knew I had to give her my solemn pledge—the one she entrusted to me when she barely knew me.

"I promise to always do my best to take care of Wesley. I will love him like my own and do anything for him forever and always."

"I know you will," she answered, barely a whisper.

> *"In case I forgot to tell you, thank you."*

And when I left that night, she said the same thing she always said after one of my visits.

"In case I forgot to tell you, thank you."

In early December, Robbin called to say Trish was quickly failing. I decided I would go down and stay overnight with her so she had the comfort of me there. But before I left to make the trek to hospice, I held Wesley on my lap.

"You know, honey, Mommy isn't doing real good. Robbin is with her now and she really thinks I ought to come right down. I want to stay with your mommy because I don't want her to be alone."

He didn't want me to go. He hated any time I was out of his sight, yet on some level, I think he understood.

By the time I got to Harrisburg, it was 9:30 p.m. and I told the staff that I wanted to sleep beside her. They moved the furniture so the recliner was nestled right next to Trish's bed. All I had to do was reach out and I could touch her. She was in and out of consciousness most of the night, but at times did open her eyes. I hummed gently, stroked her face, and held her hand.

Around five in the morning, she was drenched in perspiration and I went to ask the nurse if I could give her a bath. I nearly chuckled out loud, remembering the way Trish responded to her last one, but it was so important to me for her to be clean and not sweaty. I wanted her to be comfortable. The nurse helped me to pull the bed out and we got a basin of warm, sudsy water. This time Trish didn't move, but I just helped bathe her, finding comfort in taking care of her. We put her in a clean nightgown and placed fresh sheets on her bed. I knew Maria and Robbin were coming later on, and I wanted her to look nice. I checked in with Dan and told him I thought that maybe Trish had a day left at most. We cried together over the phone as he assured me Wesley was fine. He would be taking the kids to church and then out to eat. His role was to keep them as happy and occupied as he could while I ushered Trish into the final hours of life.

It was about ten thirty that morning, and I knew Maria would be there soon. Robbin would also be coming straight over after church, so I dozed a bit in the recliner, waiting for their arrival. Out of nowhere, I suddenly awoke with a jolt. I looked around the hospice house keenly aware that everything was all so very quiet. It was almost as though the entire facility was blanketed in peace. Trish was still in and out of consciousness, unable to talk. In that moment, I felt very strongly that I was supposed to leave and go home to my family. I had never wanted Trish to be alone, especially not during these final hours, so I was completely surprised by this undeniable gut instinct that told me I needed to go be with Wesley in this moment. After I let the nurse know I was going to leave and that Trish had some friends who would be there soon, I went back into the room to gather my things and all of a sudden, Trish's eyes opened wide. Even though she was out of it, she somehow still knew what I was doing. I went over to her bedside one last time.

"Dolly, I have to go now," I whispered.

She got restless as her arms began moving around, trying to

reach for me. I took both of her hands and gently sank down next to her on the side of her bed. She seemed very alert and I knew she was aware of everything that was happening and could hear every word I was saying.

"I love you so much," I said, meaning it with all of my heart. "I need to go home now and be with Wesley because I don't want him to be alone today. I want to be there for him."

She clung to me in those fragile seconds, not wanting to break apart, yet we both knew it was time for me to be there for the boy we both loved.

> *"This is not good-bye," I said to her. "This is just I'll see you later."*

"It's okay. This is not good-bye," I said to her. "This is just I'll see you later."

With these final words, Trish relaxed completely. It was the first time in a long while where she didn't look panicked. Instead, she tried to lean over and kiss me on the cheek. I hugged her close, and she hugged me back. Without hesitating, I rose to my feet and left the room, quite certain this was the last time I would see her this side of heaven.

As soon as I left, I called Robbin to tell her how the night had gone. I then talked to Maria, who was on her way to be with Trish. My body ached with fatigue. When I arrived home, everybody was still at church, so I showered and spent some quiet time alone in prayer, in tears, and in mourning. Through it all, I could still feel her with me, just as real as if I still had her nestled in my arms. I hoped that feeling would always stay.

After the family got home, Robbin called to say Maria was there and they both felt that Trish didn't have too much longer. Trish had been calling out Ollie's name, so Robbin asked me for his phone number. Thankfully, once we hung up, Maria was able to get Oliver on the phone so Trish could hear her brother's voice one more time. He told her it was okay to let go if she felt it was time and said his loving good-bye. Next, Trish was mumbling Wesley's name, so Robbin called me back. Dan and I quickly gathered everybody in a group. I told Wesley Mommy was about to go to heaven and if there was anything he wanted her to know, he could say it to her now through the phone.

"Hi, Mommy," his little voice said into the speaker. "I love you, Mommy. I love you lots."

He was crying as the phone then went to Jenna. "Good-bye, Trish. We love you." She mopped her spilled tears.

Anna took it next and choked, "I love you, Trish. Thank you for being my friend. We love you always."

Dan had his turn, as did the others, until finally the phone was in my hands. I ached with loss, wanting so much to have her with us still in our home. Where did the time go? How could it be the end so soon? Then again, God had blessed us with more days and memories together than anyone could have fathomed we would ever have. I had to be thankful for that.

"I love you, Dolly," I told her, pushing through my pain. I heard her raspy breathing on the other end. "Just remember we're going to be seeing you again one fine day."

The girls then gathered around the phone and, through their tears, they sang one of Trish's favorite songs, "Amazing Grace." Wesley just wanted to go into his mom's old room to be alone. Less than ten minutes later, Robbin called back to let us know that Trish had passed away.

Swallowing back my grief, I went into Trish's room to tell Wesley that Mommy went to heaven. He waited a few silent seconds, and then said, "Okay. Can I go play with Noah now?"

I told him that would be just fine. It wasn't time to console him or try to talk, hug, or hover. He'd come to me when he was ready. When he did, I would be right there waiting.

CHAPTER 27

Purple Skies

The week Trish passed was a whirlwind of activity. Everyone gathered for Trish's memorial service to honor her life, celebrate how she touched theirs, and give support to Wesley and our family. Her friends from Baltimore came, Ollie and Erin made the trip from Florida, hospice workers, my coworkers, our friends, our neighbors, our church family, and even Wesley's teacher attended to pay final respects. We propped our favorite photos of Trish around the sanctuary, which was also filled with the most glorious floral bouquets sent from so many people who loved her. Trish would have loved seeing the gorgeous arrangements. The lonely cancer patient I tended to that one shift with no one to list as a contact on her paperwork now had an outpouring of family, friends, and community. It was a remarkable sight. Pastor Mott delivered the message that Trish asked him to share. It was a message of salvation. He told everyone about the transformation that Trish had undergone and that she specifically wanted to make sure that everyone understood the change in her and why. This was not the Trish that many knew from so long ago. She had accepted Jesus into her heart and from that day forward, she was reborn and renewed. She was free. It was her hope that anyone who felt lost and alone would be inspired by her relationship with Jesus. After the eulogy, the girls sang Trish's favorite praise and worship songs. Even my little niece, Addison, got up and sang her own ultimate favorite song, "Let It Go," the theme from *Frozen*. But then Anna closed out the service with one huge surprise.

"Several months ago Trish came to me and asked for my help in writing a song for my mother," she explained to the congregation. "You see, my mom once sang and dedicated a song to her here in church, so she wanted to do the same for her. But what my mom never knew was that we secretly worked together. Trish wrote the lyrics, and I wrote the music. When she was in hospice, our project still wasn't finished. Trish called me to her bedside after my family left the room on one visit and asked me to do her a favor. She asked me to please complete the song and sing it at her service as a special gift for my mother. It's called 'God Chose You for Me,' and it's Trish's way of saying thank you, Mom, for all you've done for her."

As my daughter sang and played the piano, lifting words from Trish's heart into the air, tears rained down my face. It was the most beautiful song I had ever heard. It soothed the ache of my loss and reminded me of all the precious pieces of Trish that would always be here. They would always live on.

Several ladies were gracious enough to pull together a wonderful meal where everyone could socialize, cry, laugh, and remember good times we shared with Trish. Wesley ran about with Noah. It did my heart good. Playing seemed to be the best medicine of all for him at this point.

Cindy and George also came up for the service and helped me to put together a very special tribute. We spoke by phone days before, and Cindy wanted to do something for Wesley to honor his mother, but flowers didn't feel quite right. So we thought of a perfect plan and ordered a big bouquet of purple balloons to be delivered to the church. Before everyone left for home on that biting-cold December day, we all gathered outside for one last display of love for Trish. Our family, Ollie and Erin, along with Robbin and Maria each got a purple balloon and stood in a huddle. Wesley held on to his and would be the first one to release it. He glanced up toward his mommy's new home, and then he let the balloon go, with the rest of us following with ours. We all stood and looked heavenward, watching them lift higher and higher until they were little specks against the pale blue sky. I knew without a doubt that Trish was loving it from heaven. I smiled, imagining her saying, "Look at all the purple!" This was exactly what she would have wanted.

> *I knew without a doubt that Trish was loving it from heaven. I smiled, imagining her saying, "Look at all the purple!" This was exactly what she would have wanted.*

That night when I tucked the boys into their beds, I began with kissing Noah and saying our nightly prayer, and then worked my way down to Wesley's bunk. As he lay underneath the covers, so many emotions ran through me. What was ahead now? What kind of memories would we build together? Could I really do this? Would he ever grow to love me like a mother? I couldn't resist opening up to him a bit about the things pressing on my mind.

"You know, your mommy has been training me for a long time for this day, and I'm kind of nervous," I admitted. "Do you think I'll do a good job of taking care of you?"

He gave a small smile, so brave so soon. "I think you're going to do just great."

We then began to say the prayer we'd always shared together, a prayer I recited when I was a little girl and now shared with all of my kids at night. The one I just prayed with Noah and now was praying with my new son. His little hands folded tight as he squeezed his eyes shut. I then began reciting the verse as he followed along with me.

"And now may the Lord bless you and keep you. May His face shine upon you. May His grace, mercy, and peace flow down upon your heart, soul, and life, in the name of the Father, the Son, and the Holy Spirit. Amen." Knowing today was hard and the loss was fresh, I then asked Wesley if he'd like to add anything else to the blessing.

He nodded as if he knew just what he wanted to say. "Thank You, Lord, for hearing our prayers . . . and please help Mommy to be having a lovely time in heaven. Amen."

My insides overflowed as I tucked the blankets all around this beautiful boy who was now my son. The boy whom Trish lived for and loved more than one heart could hold. The boy God chose for our family because He knew far better than we did. The boy that would one day grow up into a man and know that his mother gave her all to provide him a happy future.

"Tricia?" Wesley asked, his voice small in the darkened room aglow by a small nightlight.

"What, honey?"

"About you being nervous . . . my mommy told me all about how God picked you for us, so that means everything will turn out just right."

A part of me melted as I touched his velvet cheek. "You know what? It already has."

"For My thoughts are not your thoughts,
Nor are your ways My ways," says the Lord.
"For as the heavens are higher than the earth,
So are My ways higher than your ways,
And My thoughts than your thoughts."

—Isaiah 55:8–9 (NKJV)

"God Chose You for Me"

by Trish Somers and Anna Seaman

When you walked into my room, I felt this sense of peace;
I knew you'd be the one to put my mind at ease.
How could I know, I was not so sure;
I just had this feeling that I'd never felt before.

God chose you for me; He knew what you could do.
I did not know how a love could be so true.
I knew you'd just be there, in my time of despair.
You came into my life; I knew you'd always be right there.

I felt so uplifted that I now had a chance;
My son and I together, both in your caring hands.
You would open up your home and open up your heart
So my little family would not be apart.

God chose you for me; He knew what you could do.
You and your family would now be mine, too.
Oh, He chose you for me because with you is where I needed to be;
With you is where I needed to be . . .

Acknowledgments

I would like to thank the many people who have been an integral part of this journey. First and most important, I want to thank my heavenly Father for saving me, for His forgiveness, and Grace. Thank You for using me and my family in a small way for the purpose of furthering Your Kingdom.

Thank you to my husband, Daniel, for loving me, for your endless support, and for being my best friend. I love you more each day, and I look forward to sharing our every tomorrow with one another. You are truly the kindest soul I have ever met.

To Anna Elizabeth—you are such a wonderful daughter and a terrific big sister to the brood! Thank you for the amazing example you are of grace and beauty. I love you, Anna. God has special plans for you!

To Jenna Abigail—it never fails to amaze me to see such compassion and gentleness in your heart. I love you dearly. You are wise beyond your years, and God has blessed you with so many gifts and talents. Thank you for your wonderful hugs and for being my little girl.

To Emma Rachel—you will forever have my gratitude for the countless glasses of ice water you brought me while I was working, for helping with your little brothers, and being just the sweet soul you are. You have such a servant's heart, and God is going to use you in amazing ways.

To Noah Daniel—Mother loves you. I am so proud of the young man you are becoming. Thank you for being strong and for learning to share me, your room, Legos, and everything! You are no longer the baby of the family, and big brother fits you well. Thank you for being so kind. You are a very special gift to me!

To Wesley—thank you for allowing us to be your family. We thank God that He saw fit to bring you into our lives. I love you as my own. I loved your mommy dearly, and she loved you more than anything in the whole world. You are such a wonderful little boy . . . so smart, loving, caring, considerate, and so funny! Your journey has not been easy, but as you grow, I pray that you will continue to see how God has guided and protected you each and every step of the way.

To Adam, Jessica, Owen, Parker, and Addy—I love you all more than words can express. Thank you for all the help, love, and support you gave us. It will always touch my heart how openly you embraced Trish and Wesley as family.

To my mom—thank you for always being there with open arms

and understanding. Trish truly loved you and adored being part of our family . . . especially when you shared the little kitties!

To Pastor Mott and Joyce and our church family at Niemonds Independent Church—you could never know what your unwavering prayers, love, calls, visits, and support meant to us. We are so grateful to everyone who provided food for our family, transportation for Trish, and assistance in any way we needed. We love each and every one of you!

To everyone at PinnacleHealth System—thank you for all of the emails and the cards I received from fellow employees all over the system. Your thoughts, prayers, and encouragement were so very appreciated.

To Kelly McCall and Andrea Becker—your kindness and thoughtfulness will never be forgotten.

To the entire staff of 1 Main Oncology—you are the most incredible group of people I have ever had the privilege to work with. I am so honored to call each of you my friend. Your support, dedication, love, and teamwork meant the world and always will. Trish loved you all. Thank you for the beautiful care you gave her.

To my nurse manager, Jackie Hunt—thank you for always believing in me. Your encouragement, kindness, support, and concern held me up more than you know.

To Dr. Lily Shah, Dr. Arlene Bobonich, and Dr. Margaret Hallahan—you will always and forever hold a special place in my heart for the kindness you gave to Trish. She absolutely had the best care possible. Each of you is an amazing physician and extraordinary person.

To our community—with more gratitude than I could ever express, I send a thank-you to everyone: friends, neighbors, Fayette Elementary School, teachers, students, classmates of the children, and local churches. We are truly blessed to live in a community that cares for one another. We were so touched by each and every card, call, visit, and countless acts of kindness extended to our family. Bless you!

To Homeland Hospice, Chrissy, Pam, and Brian—words can't convey how blessed we have been by your unwavering kindness. You were so wonderful to all of us, and we appreciate your caring and support toward our family, as well as everything you did for Trish to help keep her comfortable and to help her live life to the fullest.

To Hospice of Central Pennsylvania—to the entire staff at the Hospice Residence, you all are amazing! Thank you for the excellent care you gave Trish in her final weeks prior to her home going. She felt safe and happy there.

To Oliver and Erin Somers—thank you for your support and encouragement, as well as embracing us as part of your extended family.

To Maria Galea—thank you, Auntie Maria, for becoming our family, too! Your kindness, help, and willingness to always go the distance are something we will never forget. Trish loved you dearly. You were her best friend forever until the end of time.

To Cindy Alton—thank you for being so special and for offering such love to Trish and our entire family. We are blessed to call you and George friends.

To the "Maryland girls": Teresa, Laureen, and Sue—we so appreciate the many, many trips to Harrisburg and to McAlisterville you ladies made throughout the months of Trish's illness. You all were wonderful friends to her and to us!

To Robbin—there are no words to express my gratitude to you for all you have done. You are an angel and now the mother of furry Molly! Trish loved you so much, Robbin. Thank you for the joy you brought into her life. You are a friend forever and will eternally hold a very special place in my heart.

To Nena Madonia Oshman at Dupree-Miller—your love and belief in our story means so much. There aren't enough thank-yous for your unwavering dedication to helping to make the dream of this project a reality.

To Ami McConnell, Katie Sandell, Jonathan Merkh, and everyone at Howard Books—thank you for a phenomenal experience, for being the greatest cheerleaders along the way, and being such a joy to work with!

To Diane Nichols, one of the most amazing people I have ever had the privilege of calling my friend. Thank you for your love, caring, support, and encouragement during every step of this journey. I have loved each and every phone interview, each and every late-night emailing session, edits, and rewrites! You have been a true blessing in my life.

Acknowledgments

Special thanks go out to all of the kindhearted people worldwide who reached out to our family in support. We treasure all of the cards and letters that have been sent. I read every one of them to Trish, and they uplifted her beyond measure. We are so inspired by your love and prayers for our family, and the many new friendships that we have made along the way. May God richly bless each and every one of you.

And last, but certainly not least, to Tricia Somers. I am so thankful God gave me you. What a gift when He placed me in your path that day! Thank you for making me laugh, for showing me truly how to enjoy each moment. Thank you for the late-night talks, loads of ice cream, and lots of giggles while trying not to wake the family. You are and always will be part of our family. Thank you for entrusting Dan and me with your most precious gift . . . Romans 8:28.